BFI FILM Cl
. . . .
Rob W
S E R I E S

Colin MacCabe and David Meeker
S E R I E S   C O N S U L T A N T S

Cinema is a fragile medium. Many of the great classic films of the past now exist, if at all, in damaged or incomplete prints. Concerned about the deterioration in the physical state of our film heritage, the National Film and Television Archive, a Division of the British Film Institute, has compiled a list of 360 key films in the history of the cinema. The long-term goal of the Archive is to build a collection of perfect showprints of these films, which will then be screened regularly at the Museum of the Moving Image in London in a year-round repertory.

BFI Film Classics is a series of books commissioned to stand alongside these titles. Authors, including film critics and scholars, film-makers, novelists, historians and those distinguished in the arts, have been invited to write on a film of their choice, drawn from the Archive's list. Each volume presents the author's own insights into the chosen film, together with a brief production history and a detailed filmography, notes and bibliography. The numerous illustrations have been specially made from the Archive's own prints.

With new titles published each year, the BFI Film Classics series will rapidly grow into an authoritative and highly readable guide to the great films of world cinema.

Could scarcely be improved upon ... informative, intelligent, jargon-free companions.
The Observer

Cannily but elegantly packaged BFI Classics will make for a neat addition to the most discerning shelves.
New Statesman & Society

BFI FILM

CLASSICS

CHINATOWN

. . . .

Michael Eaton

Publishing

First published in 1997 by the
BRITISH FILM INSTITUTE
21 Stephen Street, London W1P 2LN

Reprinted 1998, 1999, 2000, 2004, 2008

The British Film Institute exists
to promote appreciation, enjoyment, protection and
development of moving image culture in and throughout the
whole of the United Kingdom.
Its activities include the National Film and
Television Archive; the National Film Theatre;
the Museum of the Moving Image;
the London Film Festival; the production and
distribution of film and video; funding and support for
regional activities; Library and Information Services;
Stills, Posters and Designs; Research;
Publishing and Education; and the monthly
Sight and Sound magazine.

British Library Cataloguing-in-Publication Data
A catalogue record for this book is available from the British Library

ISBN 0–85170–532–4
ISBN 978–0–85170–532–3

Designed by
Andrew Barron & Collis Clements Associates

Typesetting by
D R Bungay Associates, Burghfield, Berks.

Printed in Great Britain by Norwich Colour Print

CONTENTS

6   Jack Nicholson and Roman Polanski on set

'CHINATOWN'

....

Chinatown is the last, so it is often said, 'studio picture', a film which was made in a time when it was still possible for a Hollywood major to produce a complex work which, though it ultimately crashes against the rocks of despair, is never sucked into the maelstrom of cynicism. To approach it yet one more time, imagining that all its pleasures have been exhausted, that all its meanings have been disclosed, is to evoke a nostalgic memory of entering a cinema twenty years ago with an expectation so rarely experienced today.

Every film, even (perhaps especially) those that never see the light of day or the dark of night, is the result of an accident. Sometimes that contingency leads to the serendipitous discovery of a fragrant isle hitherto only alluded to in unreliable travellers' tales. More often it resembles a multi-vehicle pile-up on a rush-hour freeway. The fact that any film ever gets made at all seems more a demonstration of the operation of chaos theory than the result of rational, industrial planning. But for once the magic worked: so, *Chinatown*. It will take a while to get there.

....

It is too much of a temptation to resist the cliché 'wunderkind' when talking of Robert Evans, or to fail to evoke the shade of Irving G. Thalberg, and not only because Evans had portrayed the legendary producer in the Lon Chaney bio-pic, *The Man with a Thousand Faces* (1957). A radio actor as a child, a successful entrepreneur in the rag trade, a short-lived Hollywood juve (he had also portrayed, perhaps somewhat improbably for the son of a Jewish New York dentist, Pedro the bull-fighter in *The Sun Also Rises*, also in 1957), he had moved into independent production in the early 1960s and, by 1966, had been hired by Charles Bluhdorn of Gulf and Western as the Vice-President in Charge of Production at Paramount Studios. As he says of himself, with characteristic forbearance: 'It takes guts to be a producer, and I have guts.'[1]

The oil company was thinking of shutting down the ailing mountain and selling off the real estate to the adjoining Hollywood Cemetery before Evans turned its fortunes around with a string of box-office smashes such as *Rosemary's Baby* (1968), *Love Story* (1970) and *The Godfather* (1972), making it the number one studio in town.

In the early 70s Evans tried to negotiate a deal which would give him a percentage of the profits on every Paramount film but instead Bluhdorn proposed an unheard of offer. As Evans himself tells it, Bluhdorn said:

'I want Bob to make history ... He can make one picture a year, for five years, under his own banner, Robert Evans Productions, and still remain head of Paramount ...' [L]ike Simple Simon I fell for it ... I ended up with a kiss but no cigar.

So, for his first picture, he went to see Robert Towne: '[A] script doctor who didn't have enough money to get soles for his shoes.'[2]

An alumnus of Roger Corman's movie academy, Towne had accrued a screen credit for *Tomb of Ligeia* (1965) and had shared the card with Sam Peckinpah for *Villa Rides* (1968). By the early 70s his star was firmly in the ascendancy, not just because of his reputation as a script doctor (for Evans he had helped to fix *The Great Gatsby* in 1974 and added texture to *The Godfather*) but also because of the success of *The Last Detail* (1973). Directed by Hal Ashby, this starred Towne's old buddy, Jack Nicholson, as a sailor who, together with a black colleague, has the miserable duty of escorting a young no-hoper back to face a court-martial and a long prison sentence for a trivial offence. Made towards the end of the Vietnam war Towne's script not only pushed the envelope as far as vernacular language was concerned ('forty-seven motherfuckers' is the phrase ritualistically used) but it also depicted America, service life, masculinity and inter-racial relationships with a complexity and compassion which proved that popular American movies did not have to either ignore, condemn, patronise or pander to a young, hip, anti-authoritarian audience, but could be made from the epicentre of that very sensibility. It was a great script but it caused its writer not a little grief. He came to think that perhaps something more generic might guarantee an easier ride: 'What if I write a detective story?'[3]

Though the part was specially penned to be non-conformist icon Nicholson's crossover film as his first romantic hero, nobody at Paramount could understand the script – maybe because its sub-text concerned a theme too close to home: greed. The last time Hollywood had allowed a rogue insider to make a picture about that deadly sin, the negative had been melted down to retrieve the silver from the emulsion.

Nevertheless, Evans stuck by *Chinatown* as his choice for his first production. He was confident that Nicholson could appeal to a wider audience than the *Easy Rider* (1969) pot-heads: 'The devilish wink of his eye lit up the screen. His devastating smile shook not only the rafters but the limbs of most every woman I knew. His cracked voice did the rest.'[4] Forget his current status, in the mid-1970s Jack Nicholson was anathema to the boardrooms of conservative, corporate Paramount. But eventually Nicholson's deal was to net him $500,000 plus a percentage of the gross, an indication of his new standing in the industry as a mainstream leading man. And the producer had a director in mind – one whose name would have been guaranteed to have his fellow executives calling their stress counsellors – Roman Polanski.

Taken together, Polanski's films seem to constitute something of a test-case for what Raymond Chandler called 'the trained seals of the critical fraternity',[5] particularly those with a marked determination to balance an auteurist ball on the end of their hooters. The macabre events of this extraordinary life reveal the comfortable academic search for either consistent visual tropes or underlying thematic coherence in his work as not only a redundant but somehow also a discreditable exercise. Suddenly the critics' dictum that the work should be divorced from the life of the person who made it is exposed as a self-serving platitude.

From Polanski's childhood on the run as a renegade Jew in occupied Poland (considered as a surrealistic horror-show of European *Realpolitik*),[6] through the savage dismemberment of his pregnant wife in 60s Hollywood (considered as a twisted morality tale for a society fashionably toying with the release of its demonic genies from their repressed bottles), to his continued exile from America on an accusation of sex with a minor (considered as a long-overdue revenge drama on the *Playboy* generation), Polanski's life and work on both sides of the Berlin Wall and in the Old and the New Worlds seems to cohere into nothing more or less than a demented imago of the latter half of the 20th century.

The fact that somewhere along the way this man has made some films seems to beggar the question. Perhaps the only surprise is that he has never been asked to helm his own auto-bio-pic. So, whatever the vicissitudes of a weird and patchy directorial career in which existential art-house fare like *Knife in the Water* (1962) had preceded a British gore-fest classic like *Repulsion* (1965) and an inexplicable stinker like *Dance of the Vampires* (1967) had followed a great theatre-of-the-absurd comedy

10   The man with the knife

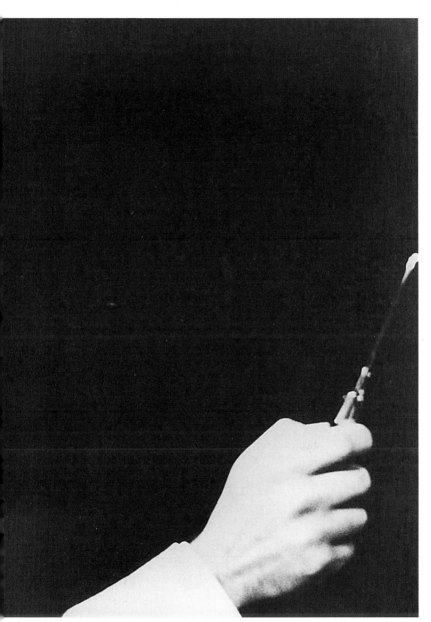

like *Cul-de-Sac* (1966), none of his critics can doubt that he has seen more of life than they ever could, far more than they would ever want to.

Suffice it to say that it was Evans who had brought this 'really offbeat' helmer of 'the drama of life' to Hollywood for *Rosemary's Baby* six years before and since that time Polanski had had two gargantuan floperoos with *Macbeth* (1971) and *What?* (1973).

These days Robert Towne graciously acknowledges Polanski's contribution to the script that was eventually filmed, even going so far as to call him the best collaborator he ever worked with. At the time of rewriting, though, things were rather different, with Towne evidently and understandably threatened by an outsider's lack of respect for the script he considered his best work heretofore.

From today's perspective, however, the clash of Towne and Polanski seems a marriage if not Heavenly then at least Beverley (Hills, that is). It seems that it was not just the director's insistence on streamlining and simplifying the epic narrative that turned out to be so significant but the insistence on a specific point of view that structures the way the story is told that made *Chinatown* such a classically composed work.

It is an industry maxim that there are always a million reasons to turn down a movie and it is an industry truism that it is only the obsessive drive of one individual that can get a picture off the launch pad. That individual is (and I say this with some reluctance) very rarely the writer. But neither is it all that often (for those critics in the auditorium and theorists in the academy who still, for the most part, seem more settled if they can name and nail a *fons et origino* to celebrate or castigate) the director, either. In the case of *Chinatown* it seems evident that the individual who quite simply made this film happen, even if he cannot be credited with weaving its complex web of meanings, was the producer.

. . . .

Before any image, the music: 'eerie, haunting, mysterious ... a lonely horn ... a solo trumpet played against strings'[7] – but even that became the subject of argument, rancour and lasting ill-feeling between the producer and the director. After, according to Evans, a disastrous audience preview out in the sticks at San Luis Obispo, where real people apparently must live, he made the unilateral decision to junk the original soundtrack composed by Polanski's 'rinkydink friend' and hire the ever-dependable Jerry Goldsmith to save the picture: 'his theme was so erotic

and eerie that magically *Chinatown* became mesmerising'. Then, over a
sepia-tinted monochromatic Art Deco design which evokes early sound
cinema, that enigmatic title – the first puzzle we have to solve, perhaps
the last we will. Evans to Towne:

> '...What's it called?'
> '*Chinatown*'.
> 'What's that got to do with it. You mean it's set in Chinatown?'
> 'No. "Chinatown" is a state of mind – Jake Gittes's fucked-up state
> of mind.'
> 'I see,' I said, not seeing it at all.[8]

It's amazing that the title stayed. Towne got the idea from a Hungarian
vice-cop who had once worked the Chinatown beat and whom the writer
met when he bought a dog from him – his sheepdog, Hira, who would,
as it happens, later be immortalised in the screenplay credit for *Greystoke*
when Towne, axiomatically disappointed with the distance between his
mental fantasy and the cinematic reality as only a screenwriter can be,
took his own name off the picture.

'You don't know who's a crook and who isn't a crook,' said the cop. 'So
in Chinatown they say: just don't do a goddamned thing.'[9] For Towne
'Chinatown' became a synecdoche for the entire City of Los Angeles, a place
where you have no idea what's going on [10] and where it's best to let it alone for
good or ill. So the film's title is a metaphor for a city which itself often seems
more metaphorical than actual. Mike Davis has made the point well:

> Los Angeles ... is ... a stand-in for capitalism in general. The
> ultimate world significance – and oddity – of Los Angeles is that
> it has come to play the double role of utopia *and* dystopia for
> advanced capitalism.[11]

This was a metaphor Roman Polanski had trouble coming to terms with
when Evans first gave him the script:

> Called *Chinatown* despite its total absence of oriental location or
> characters, it simply couldn't have been filmed as it stood, though
> buried somewhere in its 180-plus pages was a marvellous movie ...
> *Chinatown* was a great title, but unless we set at least one scene in

L.A.'s real-life Chinatown, we'd be cheating – pulling in the public under false pretences.[12]

The writer, the producer, the director – all at each other's throats before the picture was even in pre-production. 'Chinatown' – that place where no one ever knows what's going on – might rather be a metaphor for movie-making.

. . . .

The first images are of black and white still photographs flipped over like a 'What the Butler Saw' peep-show: pictures of a man and a woman engaging in passionate, but furtive intercourse – their clothes are rumpled, the man still wears his hat – coupling outside of the social world, in the woods. From the very first moments of the film two of its orchestrating themes are introduced: illicit sexuality and voyeurism. Even though the clothes in the stills are from the 30s the very explicitness of their content announced the film, at the time of its release, as incontrovertibly 'modern', the product of a Hollywood cinema at a time when censorship codes were being tested, allowing for a more 'adult' cinema. Before any moving characters are seen moanings are heard, but these are not the orgasmic grunts of the man in the picture but the groans of the cuckolded husband before he throws the photos into the air in disgust.

Impassively watching, unmoved by this display of agony, sits a wiseacre who quips: 'Enough is enough, Curly. You can't eat the venetian

1 4   Illicit sexuality and voyeurism: 'what kind of guy do you think I am?'

blinds, I just had them installed on Wednesday.' He is instantly defined, not only by his sardonic manner but by his beautifully tailored white suit and the sumptuous decor of his office with its wood-panelled fitted bar, as a prosperous professional in control of himself and his surroundings, capable, confident, cock-sure. Events which threaten the precarious domestic stability of his clients are all in a day's work for him.

As he leads Curly out of the office we learn more about him: this is a man who spies on people for money and is unashamed. He makes a good living, he has a classy-looking secretary, he employs two well-dressed operatives and he is not short of clients. For another one, a Mrs Mulwray, is waiting to see him. By leaving this minor character, Curly, in the private eye's debt, the script initiates an imperceptibly perfect 'set-up' which will be 'paid off' towards the very end of the film: 'I don't want your last dime. What kind of a guy do you think I am?' Presumably that's what we'll find out.

Thus are we introduced to the normal world of Jake Gittes and the status that he occupies at the beginning of the tale. Already we might predict that this well-established and secure position will be troubled before the story is through.

Mrs Mulwray is just another client, even though Jake feigns shock at the thought that her husband is 'involved' with another woman. A character from outside enters his world and offers just another assignment which will kick off the story, which will incite the action, the drama.

Not untypically at this stage in the tale Jake counsels caution: 'Let sleeping dogs lie … You're better off not knowing' – a sentiment whose significance and irony is not yet apparent and, of course, if the lady had taken his advice there would be no story at all. Everything is routine; the only difference is that the object of this inquiry is a prominent public figure – Hollis Mulwray, chief engineer of water and power.

So, in just a few short minutes the world of the film, the dominant character traits of the protagonist, the central problematic of the first act (Jake has to dig the dirt on Mulwray's infidelity) and the genre (the detective story with its investigative structure) have all been elegantly and seamlessly delineated.

No paying guest comes cold to the welcoming glow of any movie. The pleasure of all popular narrative depends upon a recognised play between repetition and difference, between recognition and originality. For an audience at the time this film was made these first two opening scenes already employ both a knowledge of the screen persona of the star for whom the part was especially written ('Jake Gittes handles people the same way Jack does, alternately intimidating and coaxing. He has Jack's ability to manipulate people in a funny and reflective manner'[13]) and an awareness of some, at least, of the contours of the type of story this is, the determinants of the private eye genre, involving a species of narrative organisation to which any audience will undoubtedly, whether they know it or not, have already been exposed.

. . . .

Show me a man or woman who cannot stand mysteries and I will show you a fool, a clever fool – perhaps – but a fool just the same.[14]

The Private Eye is the perfect existential hero for a species of story-telling whose central quest involves investigation and the pursuit of knowledge. He (still most often and, of course, in this instance) is approached in his office by someone from the outside world and sent out into that world. Already we have a basic topography, dramaturgy and *dramatis personae*. The investigator is our surrogate, bold as we are cautious. He has a reason to poke his nose into and to overhear the gossip from all strata of society on our behalf, for we are as keen to know the answer to an enigma as he is. The Earholing Eye is Nosy – all three monkeys in one. And, because the P.I. is an independent operative, he need not (like the compromised policeman) function as a representative of an impersonal, bureaucratic or even malevolent authority – he cannot be gainsaid in his search for truth in a world of dissemblance.

The Private Investigator is an urban creature, he can negotiate the maze that is the city and crack its codes. The genre which tells his tales originated in the early half of the 19th century alongside the growth of the modern, anonymous metropolis where prior community values were heated and dissolved in the refiner's fire. A place where no man knows his neighbour and criminal acts can be committed without ever being noticed, where a veil can be drawn over even the most heinous of atrocities. In this complex conurbation the detective was created to restore some semblance of temporary order to the unintelligible chaos of life, to return with a reassurance that the world can make sense, it can be read, and that good can triumph over evil.

Two years before the word 'detective' even appeared in the English language the investigative genre was inaugurated by Edgar Allan Poe through the creation of his master of 'ratiocination', C. Auguste Dupin.[15] As Poe so clearly put it, the detective exists 'to play the Oedipus'. Was he thinking of that intellectually triumphant Oedipus at the moment when he solved the riddle of the Sphinx (a conundrum whose answer, of course, is the nature of our species) or of that Oedipus at the *dénouement* of the tragedy, when, as literature's first detective, he has embarked on a quest to uncover who is responsible for the plague in his city and has come to the tragic realisation that to unmask the guilty party he need do no more than look in a mirror – that the cause of the social calamity is his own unknown illicit and incestuous sexual activity?

It is, naturally, those fictional private detectives operating in the period in which *Chinatown* is set (*c.* 1937), though, who provide a more direct pedigree for Jake Gittes. In both film and literature in the 1930s the 'detective story business in general', to use Chandler's phrase, was beneath critical consideration by those opinion-forming trained seals. Its sociological perspicacity eluded most contemporary commentators and P.I. pics, even when made by major studios, remained bottom-of-the-bill B-picture fodder.

They were often series pictures churned out mechanistically and usually involving a particular detective hero derived from, though not necessarily following the contours of, a literary source: the Saint, Charlie Chan; even, of course, Sherlock Holmes. This was unsurprising given their short story origins and the dramaturgical essence of the premise (client approaches detective with a mystery to solve – a formula ripe for constant, serial repetition). But, with their short running time, their fast turn around and their limited budgets, the films which featured them could command few of the resources of script, cast or *mise en scène* accorded to the A-picture.

A similar situation prevailed in the publishing industry where, for instance, Dorothy L. Sayers could make the confident and matronising assertion that the detective story, which made her as embarrassed as it made her rich, 'does not, and by hypothesis never can, attain the loftiest level of literary achievement'.[16] But Chandler argued that there was one writer in particular of this form which seemed to be universally acknowledged as debased who had transcended mere dime-novel popularity, not only because of his style but also because of his content – someone who 'wrote or tried to write *realistic* mystery fiction'.[17] That 'first-class writer' was the former Pinkerton detective Dashiell Hammett.

But in spite of Hammett's 'Continental Op' tales and his four great novels, it was down to Chandler to create a series of novels beginning with *The Big Sleep*, published in 1939, which would irrevocably move the mystery story from pulp obsolescence to literary Parnassus with the creation of his first-person protagonist, Philip Marlowe. Marlowe is a small-business man, directing his rage against the decadent, moneyed élite who pay his wages ($25 dollars per diem plus expenses) to which he can only aspire to belong. Yet he is equally fearful of the abyss populated by a working class which is ethnically complicated and into which he could so easily be sucked.

In 'The Simple Art of Murder', Raymond Chandler says: 'It is not a very fragrant world, but it is the world you live in, and certain writers with tough minds and a cool spirit of detachment can make very interesting and even amusing patterns out of it.' So he's setting up a dialectic – and how Chandler would have hated that concept – between real life and story-telling. He goes on to evoke, in his nostalgic cups, a religious symbolism: 'In everything that can be called art there is a quality of redemption …' – put that on hold, as Chandler himself does, for the meanwhile. Then, memorably, he evokes a world and introjects his hero into it:

> But down these mean streets a man must go who is not himself mean, who is neither tarnished nor afraid. The detective in this kind of story must be such a man. He must be a complete man and a common man and yet an unusual man. He is the hero, he is everything … He must be the best man in his world and a good enough man for any world. I do not care much about his private life … I think he might seduce a duchess and I am quite sure he would not spoil a virgin … If there were enough like him I think the world be a very safe place to live in, and yet not too dull to be worth living in.

Maybe the director of *Repulsion* could have learnt something from the prelapsarian sexual morality of that alumnus of Dulwich College.

It was a photo-essay in *New West* magazine on 'Raymond Chandler's L.A.' that provided the mythical genesis for Towne to locate his detective story in the Los Angeles of the 1930s,[18] but it is obvious that his creation is more of an argument with rather than a simple homage to Chandler's romantic knight of the city and Hammett's cynical embodiment of capitalist commodity fetishistic social relationships.

Unlike Chandler's hero, Jake is not a lone wolf located in a scummy Hollywood rented office, he doesn't take his liquor from a cheap half-pint secreted in his filing cabinet and he doesn't look down his nose on divorce cases – they are mother's milk and father's meat and drink to him. 'J. J. Gittes was no pale, down-at-heel imitation of Marlowe. Robert Towne had conceived him as a glamorous, successful operator, a snappy dresser with a coolly insolent manner – a new archetypal detective figure.'[19]

It is, therefore, illuminating to compare Towne's original creation with two adaptations of Chandler's novels made around the same time as *Chinatown*. Robert Altman's version of a late Philip Marlowe novel (*The Long Goodbye* was published in 1953 and made into a movie twenty years later) throws Elliott Gould as Chandler's tarnished, hard-boiled but soft-centred urban Galahad into a contemporary milieu where his values and morality seem quaint and obsolete: a total anachronism, useless if not laughable. Chandler himself had written to his agent of this book: 'I

Elliott Gould in *The Long Goodbye*

Robert Mitchum in *Farewell, My Lovely*

didn't care *whether the mystery was fairly obvious* [italics in the original], but I cared about the people, about the strange corrupt world we live in, and how any man who tried to be honest looks in the end either sentimental or plain foolish.'[20]

Altman and his scenarist (Leigh Brackett, by the way, one of the old-time scribes of Hawks's *The Big Sleep*, 1946) take that sentiment and revel in it, deconstructing the genre just as Peckinpah did with the Western in *Pat Garrett and Billy the Kid* in the same year and Dick Lester did for Robin Hood in *Robin and Marion* three years later. It is as if all these 70s films are not only disdainful of the characteristics of the traditional hero but set out to take issue with the very contours of traditional Hollywood genres. (I'd best not even mention Arthur Penn's *Night Moves* [1975], scripted by Alan Sharp, or Coppola's *The Conversation* from the same year as *Chinatown*, as both of these brilliant films refuse, in their own particular ways, the very possibility of not only the investigator but investigation itself.)

Farewell, My Lovely, directed by Dick Richards in 1975, is, on the other hand and at the very same time, an entirely loving, if not reverential, Chandler adaptation. Casting Robert Mitchum as an unreconstructed romantic, this movie never questions Chandler's values, indeed in its urge to re-evoke war-time L.A., it strives to embody a nostalgia for them.

Chinatown, template in waiting, pursues neither of these extreme options. It doesn't throw out the conventional contours of either the private eye hero or the classic structure of the investigation plot, but unashamedly parades its knowledge of and respect for them. But neither does it painstakingly try and re-create a type of movie-making imbued with a moral code which seemed, at the time of Vietnam and Watergate, not only entirely obsolete but a deceitful fabrication. Rather, through the subtle and knowing changes Towne and Polanski make in the characterisation of the detective hero and the ultimate impossibility of his quest, *Chinatown* tells a story which was absolutely modern, which was so much a product of its time, even though it is set nearly forty years before and even though it more than repays repeated viewings twenty years later. It is a story which says that, sure, wrongs can ultimately be *uncovered* but the seeker after truth is not only completely incapable of righting them but his very search will only make matters worse.

. . . .

In the film's next sequence Jake sets out to stalk his prey. The Mayor, in an address to a public meeting, introduces another of the crucial organising systems of the film: water, and its contrary, drought: 'Los Angeles is a desert community … Beneath our streets is a desert.' Jake yawns and reads the racing pages (is this show of boredom Polanski's coded attack on Towne's fascination with the hydraulic history of the city?). The Mayor presents a proposal for a dam to be paid for by a public bond but this is determinedly opposed by Hollis Mulwray, from Water and Power. Jake finally takes notice as the bespectacled, lanky, precise man wearing a bow-tie tells the politicians that he refuses to build the dam because it is of the same dangerous design as another dam, the Van der Lip, which once burst its banks, killing five hundred people. It is not only the boosterist Mayor who Mulwray rankles as an irate farmer leads in a flock of sheep and confronts the engineer with an accusation that somebody must be paying him to divert water from the farms in the valley. It is evident that Mulwray has his enemies. There is also the suspicion planted that he is somehow embroiled in political corruption.

Jake shadows Mulwray, watching through binoculars which blank out the eyes, as he inspects a dried-up river course. Gittes tails him to an out-flow pipe by the ocean and waits as day turns to night, the first night scene in the film, when the first untoward event occurs in this routine investigation. A stream of water comes suddenly cascading down the channel and into the Pacific. He follows Mulwray to a reservoir, pausing to remove a flyer urging a 'Yes' vote for the dam bond from his windshield: Los Angeles is dying of thirst. With a neat piece of professional methodology Jake places what in a folk tale would be a 'magical agent' but here is just a cheap watch under the back wheel of Mulwray's car. Its smashed face effects a transition back into Gittes's office and indicates that the engineer had remained at the reservoir all night. As his operative Walsh exclaims: 'This guy's got water on the brain.'

. . . .

If one stopped the flow of water here for three days the jackals would reappear and the sand of the desert.[21]

Considering how many films have been made *in* Los Angeles it is amazing how few of them have been *about* the history of this strange megalopolis on the furthest edge of western expansion, hemmed in by mountains, desert and the Pacific Ocean. *Chinatown* is also unlike the majority of those films which do have La-La land's past as some kind of a background in being concerned with neither the mythology of the movie business, nor with historic criminals from LAPD files. Neither is it an historical film which is based upon a classic L.A. novel, as, for example, *They Shoot Horses, Don't They?* (1969), *Day of the Locust* (1975) or *True Confessions* (1981). *Chinatown*, instead, is an original screenplay about the political and economic past of the writer's home town, penned, significantly, by the son of a Southern California realtor.

However, the historical events depicted in the film have been condensed and transposed to the late 30s from an earlier epoch – the first quarter of the 20th century. So it is worth taking a short and simplified detour through L.A.'s aqueous history in order to see how Towne synthesised and syncretised actual historical events into fiction.

> Here is an artificial city which has been pumped up under forced draught, inflated like a balloon, stuffed with rural humanity like a goose with corn ... It has never imparted an urban character to its

'Beneath our streets is a desert'

incoming population for the simple reason that it never had any urban character to impart. On the other hand, the place has retained the manners, culture and general outlook of a huge, country village.[22]

Surrounded by cattle ranches Los Angeles had a population of a mere 11,000 in 1880 but by 1904 this had already risen to above 200,000. This desert town, characterised today by its individually owned outdoor swimming pools and well-sprinkled lawns, had little local water supply and had quickly outgrown that meagre capacity. The solution to this problem was in the hands of William Mulholland, superintendent of a private water company which was purchased by the city in 1904.[23] With the former Mayor of L.A., one Fred Eaton, the pioneering Mulholland set out to find a constant, replenishable source of water, travelling as far as the Owens Valley, 250 miles north east of the burgeoning city, on the edge of the High Sierras. The fresh water which ran from these mountains could, potentially, be piped into L.A. solely by gravity through what would become the largest aqueduct in the world. So, in spite of the protests of the Owens Valley farmers, Eaton began his machinations to get hold of the water rights which he could lease for the City of Los Angeles, arguing that the Owens River water could amply supply both a population ten times the size that his city was at the turn of the century as well as allowing more than sufficient run off for the local agricultural population in the valley in perpetuity.

But before this scheme was even made public the backroom chicanery of the city fathers began. A syndicate of local business men, including Harrison Otis, publisher of the L.A. *Times*, and Henry Huntington, owner of what was then the largest urban public transport fleet in the world (a fact which often surprises present-day visitors to Southern California as the inadequacy of its bus system these days is legendary), initiated a clandestine land grab, obtaining thousands of acres at a knock-down price in the San Fernando Valley, immediately to the north of the city, through which Mulholland's aqueduct would inevitably have to run. Also, to protect their investment in the Sierras, the Angelenos contrived to have national forest boundaries extended into the Owens Valley, curtailing the farmers' possibilities of expansion.

In November 1913, to much triumphalist ballyhoo, the inaugurating ceremony of the aqueduct took place in the San Fernando

Valley, now transformed from worthless scrub to immensely valuable agricultural land on the edge of a city which was growing exponentially. Mulholland made his famous and taciturn speech as the Owens River water cascaded into L.A.: 'There it is. Take it!'

With their pockets well-lined the city fathers began the process of extending the streetcar system and incorporating communities in the San Fernando Valley into the city – 'bringing', as a *Chinatown* character will say, 'the city to the water'. There now seemed to be no limits on the expansion of Los Angeles. By the 20s the San Fernando Valley alone could have used up nearly all the water from the aqueduct. But, in his hubristic zeal to complete his monumental feat of engineering in record time, Mulholland had neglected to build a reservoir of sufficient capacity to store water for use in dry years when there was not enough for both the insatiable residents of the city and the small farmers 250 miles away. So when land agents from L.A. began a process of secretly buying up more of the water rights in the Sierras and the Water Department tried to cut a channel to divert the water away from the farmers' land the Owens Valley residents finally went to war.

Over the next few years the inhabitants of the Owens Valley led a campaign of sabotage: concrete ditches and conduit pipes were dynamited and city employees held up at gunpoint and run out of the region whenever they fronted up. The spokesmen and defenders of the interests of the agricultural community were the aptly named Watterson brothers. They cannot simply be seen as the peoples' heroes but bank-owners not above a spot of chicanery themselves. They demanded that the city buy out the entire district but this time at inflated prices, provide reparations for those families who had already sold up their farms and, with amazing foresight, compensate the community by supplying the infrastructure that would allow the development of the region for tourism. Los Angeles seemed to be held to ransom but Mulholland's department fought back, transporting a heavily armed company of war veterans into the area to protect his beloved aqueduct.

But the battle was won not by this militia but by accountants. A state banking regulator discovered that the Wattersons had been cooking the books of their banks, shunting around the farmers' savings fraudulently to hide the losses from their own dubious investments. This earned the brothers a trip to San Quentin and left the residents betrayed and demoralised.

The 'Rape of the Owens Valley' was now complete, the pockets of the speculators lined by judicious use of insider knowledge and complete domination of the southern Californian political system and Los Angeles could continue to boosterise its fictional self as an earthly paradise for wealthy Anglo immigrants only and a union-free zone for expansionist entrepreneurs. And, when in 1928 the Mulholland-designed St Francis Dam burst apart destroying over a thousand homes and taking nearly five hundred lives, the dead and homeless were mostly Mexican citrus workers, 'for the Mexicans, of course, were permitted to live in the pathway of possible floods'.[24]

. . . .

So this sordid and protracted tale of capitalist greed and political machination, more than likely erased from the memory of most contemporary Angelenos in this fundamentally amnesiac and contractually transformative of ecologies, forms the background to *Chinatown*. It is tempting to see Mulholland as the prototype for Hollis Mulwray and Noah Cross as a conflation of all the members of the business syndicate who benefited from the engineer's obsessive, public-spirited zeal.

But Towne was too much of a native himself to realise that neither a local history lesson nor a polemic on water and power would stand any chance of being sellable as a screenplay. These all too real estate crimes are not movie crimes. So the writer transformed an unsellable history which clearly outraged him into a pitchable genre yarn. The economic history of a polluted Poisonville becomes channelled into a universal flow, something a movie executive, perhaps even an audience, could understand: a tale about a guy and a gal.

Mulholland's name remains immortalised by the beautiful, serpentine drive which winds its way along the crest of the Hollywood Hills allowing spectacular, familiar movie views (which would have been entirely unfamiliar to the eponymous engineer) over both the smog-heavy suburban sprawl of the San Fernando Valley and the apparently earthquake-proof high-rises of downtown L.A. This is real estate in which most of the world's population wishes it could invest.

And this is where, it almost goes without saying, Jack Nicholson had a house that Polanski lodged in during the rewrites of *Chinatown*. Maybe it was the vista from Mulholland Drive that Polanski was thinking of when he wrote of L.A.: 'There's no more beautiful city in the world … provided it's seen by night and from a distance.'[25] Or perhaps he was rather recalling the prospect from the rented house on Cielo Drive where his wife, Sharon Tate, and three of their friends had been murdered by members of the Manson family only five years before *Chinatown*. No, maybe it was, after all, Nicholson's house he was recalling – that place where, according to the Los Angeles District Attorney's office, he allegedly drugged and had coercive sex with a thirteen-year-old girl two years after.

. . . .

Walsh's photographs show an altercation between Mulwray and an older man in which the words 'apple core' have been overheard. Even though neither the audience nor the detective has been introduced to this character, we perhaps have sufficient experience in story-telling to suspect that there is no such thing as extraneous information. Tales, unlike life, are not permeated by meaningless noise; like dreams there is nothing in them which cannot be interpreted, even if erroneously. As Chekhov sort of put it, if we see a gun on the wall in the first act then we know it will be fired in the third. So Jake's patronising dismissal of

'I make an honest living'

'This business requires a certain amount of finesse'

Walsh's evidence because it seems not to be immediately pertinent to the extra-marital inquiry ('This business requires a certain amount of finesse') already might appear short-sighted. The very fact that the hero sees nothing of significance in this figure might alert us (certainly it will scream out to us on a second viewing) that this character, and the shadow that he casts across the lives of the other characters in the tale, is determinant.

The solution to the problem has been presented to the detective at the very start of the story, but as yet he doesn't even know what the problem is. So the central theme of voyeurism and its contrary, blindness, is already paraded, although we will only realise this in retrospect as the narrative unravels: *Chinatown* is not simply about seeing, it is about seeing wrongly – the answer is in front of Gittes's eyes (or nose) but he is blind to it.

This narrative trope cannot but recall *The Purloined Letter*. In Poe's story the object of a search, a missing letter whose contents could destabilise a nation, is hidden in the most obvious of places: a letter rack. But here the investigator, Dupin, is smart enough to see it.

The narrative journey recommences after this temporary stalling with a call from Jake's other operative, Duffy. Mulwray has been spotted ('he's found himself some cute little twist, the old buzzard'): he's on a rowboat on the lake in Echo Park – more water! So Jake joins Duffy to snap the couple and Gittes catches his first sight of the girl whom he, wrongly of course, sees as his lover. Jake tails them to an apartment house where the image of this very young, blonde girl ingenuously modelling a virginal white dress is reflected in the long, phallic lens of his prying camera as she kisses her aged protector. And it is this image which, framed in a heart-shaped border, finds its way onto the front page of the paper under the headline: 'Department of Water Blows, Chief's Use of Funds for Love Nest …' and is read by Jake in a barber's chair as his face is lathered by the barber who admires his 'blasé' reaction to the ensuing publicity – 'You're practically a movie star.'

The typically garrulous barber makes more than small talk about the weather – 'this heat's murder' – as outside the window, decentred and out of focus, steam pours out of a car's radiator, showing what will happen to water if it's put under pressure and overheated: it will blow.

As Jake also does when another customer impugns his habitual practice of sticking his nose into other people's affairs and destroying

lives for money. He counters: 'I make an honest living' and attacks this banker for his professional conduct: foreclosing mortgages and making families homeless. He is only calmed down by the barber defusing the situation with an off-colour joke, particularly appropriate for the divorce dick as it concerns some man 'who's tired of screwing his wife' and in which the first oriental reference of the film is contained when this guy-in-the-gag is advised: 'Why don't you do what the Chinese do?'

Jake is proud and defensive of his occupation. Presumably, for him, this routine assignment is now over and he awaits the arrival of yet another client to kick off yet another matrimonial investigation, but this, of course, is not to be. Jake's normality and the confidence he has in his position are about to be forever shattered.

He returns to the office anxious to repeat the joke to his operatives and sends his receptionist, Sophie, out of the arena of masculine bonding to 'the little girl's room'. Towne has said that he used the naked racism of the joke as a way of characterising Gittes's attitude to ethnic difference as being emblematic of the time and as an efficient way of encoding a whole nexus of Jake's attitudes towards women, that certain things cannot be said by men in front of them, again appropriate to a man of the 1930s. This is clearly effective as, certainly for today's audience, Jake's enthusiastic pleasure at this tale reveals our distance from him. Even though he is our protagonist, our surrogate, we are distanced from him here – but not just because of a joke.

The 'story' concerns 'this guy' who follows the advice of his friend in enlivening his sagging domestic sexual life by imitating the

Chinese style of screwing which, in the world of the tale, involves habitually stopping *in media res*. The punchline, at which Jake explodes orgasmically, involves the wife exclaiming: 'Hey, what's the matter with you? You're screwing just like a Chinaman!' This exposes her direct, experiential knowledge of this exotic mode of congress, of which her husband has only just been told, and by another fellow at that, indirectly revealing him as a naive cuckold.[26] Having expelled a woman from the scene, Jake rides roughshod over the attempts of his employees to stop his 'story', revealing himself not only as someone who cannot see correctly but as someone who doesn't know when to listen.

The reason for their embarrassment is soon revealed when, with Jake's face in foreground close-up, the door to his inner office opens and the figure of a woman dressed in a classy powder-blue outfit with an imperious demeanour appears, unseen by him. It is a figure any movie-goer will recognise, the other star name of the picture, Faye Dunaway.[27]

Star entrances are so important in movies and this one, at first sight, seems so simple, barely choreographed. The door behind Jake opens and she steps into frame, slightly out of focus, never moving, no emotion on her face, her size diminished in comparison to his dominating close-up and continual facial movements. The simple shot is held throughout most of the recounting of the joke, interrupted only by a brief cut-away to show the gurning embarrassment of Duffy and Walsh which gradually turns into smirking superiority. Towne wanted to show that Gittes is exposed as a cheap 'pimp in a suit, when a woman

She's behind you!

of class and substance appears'. But it is evident that this scene does far more than that.

The seeming simplicity of this set-up is, in fact, far more marked in the context of the film's directorial system than any elaborate entrance could ever be. For this is the first instance (and one of only a very few times in the entire film) when the audience is given a different and a superior access to knowledge from that of the protagonist.

Though Towne has said: '*Chinatown*, I think, is the only detective movie of its length in which there is never a break from Gittes's point of view... You are with him shot for shot from the beginning to the end ...',[28] he is misremembering. For a few short moments, through this simple camera set-up, we know something that Jake Gittes does not. This differential access to information is, incidentally, clearly signalled in the script (where Towne writes: 'A stunning young woman appears behind Gittes in his doorway ... unseen by Gittes') and is compounded by that reaction shot of the two operatives. Like Duffy and Walsh, we are, for once, let in on the secret before our hero finds out.

Though this is a common device in most films, I repeat that it is the first time it happens here and it breaks the flow of the narration in the most disturbing and dynamic manner without drawing attention to itself in any underlined or expressionistic manner.

. . . .

It is the duty of writers to be omniscient about the story world they have created and the characters who people it. It is one of the most important (and mind-bending) of their tasks, therefore, to orchestrate exactly what their characters need to know at any particular point in the story and to be in control of just how much is revealed to their audience and when. I call this, I hope not too pretentiously, the choreography of knowledge. Who knows what, when, why and how?

Structurally, there are only three possible options for the writer in dealing with the relationship between the protagonist and the audience in regard to what is known:

(i) the audience can know exactly what the protagonist knows, and no more nor less;
(ii) the audience can know less than the protagonist knows; or
(iii) the audience can know more than the protagonist knows.

The third of the above options – where the audience knows more than the character(s) in the scene – is what constitutes classic Hitchcockian suspense.[29] The same set of determinants operates, of course, with respect to the relationship between the protagonist and any of the other characters in the drama. The writer needs to work out painstakingly who knows what at any particular moment and how they found out, so, one way or another, the protagonist can find it out from them.

Most films, of course, deploy all three strategies at particular points in the course of the narrative. Hitchcock's own *North by Northwest* (1959) is a clear and instructive example of how this movement between levels of knowledge can work. For the first act of the tale we, the audience, are as ignorant of what is going on as is the protagonist, Roger Thornhill (Cary Grant). From the moment when he is abducted, when he foils an attempt on his life, when he realises he must be a victim of mistaken identity and tries to find out who the real 'George Caplan' is, to the point when he appears to the world as the murderer of a diplomat at the United Nations and so must flee for his life from both the bad guys and the police, Thornhill has no idea what is going on – and neither do we.

Then the action in New York is left behind and there is an establishing shot of a brass plaque bearing the title: United States Intelligence Agency in which is reflected the Capitol building. Once inside we are allowed to eavesdrop on the government agents who discuss what has really been happening. Caplan is a decoy; he doesn't really exist, he has been created to distract the enemy spies from the existence of a real agent who has infiltrated the organisation. So, at the start of the second act we know (almost) everything and Thornhill still knows nothing. We have become the spectators of a classic Hitchcockian *suspense* drama.

The third act is inaugurated when the Professor rescues Thornhill, brings him up to speed on what we already know and fills him in on what we didn't know for sure, but perhaps had suspected: that the woman who apparently saved him on the train and with whom he fell in love, but who then seemed to be revealed as the villain's mistress who set him up to be wiped out, is really the government agent. So we are returned to the same state as we were in the beginning: the audience and the protagonist know exactly the same. But not for long. For, shortly after the plot takes Thornhill to Rapid City, Dakota, he confronts the woman who, apparently to protect her cover in the eyes of the villain, shoots our hero dead in a crowded cafeteria. This is a real shock for us; we had been lulled into thinking that we knew what was going on. However, in the very next scene the Professor drives out to meet his agent in a secluded spot and it is revealed to us that Thornhill is really still alive, the bullets were blanks and Eve was in on the act all along. So, for this short sequence the audience (for the only time in the narrative) have been placed in the position of knowing *less* than the protagonist. We were *surprised* by the shooting. But Hitchcock doesn't like to leave us in this position of being duped for very long. For the rest of the picture we are returned to the same position of knowledge as our protagonist and, at the end of the film, he (and we) know everything.

The example of *North by Northwest* shows how, in classic thriller film narration, a carefully choreographed movement between the three levels of knowledge can operate. It would be difficult to think of a film in which the audience knew less than the protagonist throughout without our rebelling against such an insufferable know-all – nobody loves a clever dick. When such mighty intellects as Auguste Dupin and his ever paler progeny such as Sherlock Holmes or Hercule Poirot are let loose on a conundrum they usually start out, like us, knowing nothing, although there always comes a time when the great detective has put all the pieces together while we are still in the dark. Perhaps that is why in such whodunits the protagonists are usually accompanied by a dim sidekick, a Watson – not only so there is a character to whom they can explain their intellectually superior reasoning but also to act as a surrogate for the audience.

Equally, it would be hard to think that we could watch a film where we knew more than the protagonists throughout – where we were the clever dicks – without losing all empathy for the hero and the jeopardy in which he/she has been placed. Both of those narrative strategies seem like species of sadism. In the former the story-telling rubs our noses in our own ignorance and in the latter we watch as the protagonist suffers tortures for our entertainment.

However, in both literary and filmic narration, the strategy of having the audience and the protagonist know exactly the same – we find out as he or she finds out – is not uncommon. Indeed, it is a strategy that seems particularly appropriate for the private eye story and which is present in the first-person narration of, among those of many others, the novels of Chandler which were a conscious point of departure for *Chinatown*.

In the 1946 adaptation of Chandler's *The Lady in the Lake*, directed by Robert Montgomery, this was taken to its illogical conclusion with the eye of the protagonist fused with the lens of the camera so that the audience only saw the face and figure of Philip Marlowe (also played by Montgomery) when it was reflected in a mirror, a puddle or some other shiny surface. Chandler was characteristically scathing about this gimmicky literalisation of the literary notion of first-person point of view:

> The camera eye technique of *Lady in the Lake* is old stuff in Hollywood. Every young writer or director has wanted to try it. 'Let's make the camera a character'; it's been said at every lunch table in Hollywood one time or another. I knew one fellow who wanted to make the camera the murderer; which wouldn't work without an awful lot of fraud. The camera is too honest.[30]

From what we know from the gossip surrounding the pre-production of *Chinatown*, perhaps Polanski's greatest contribution to the structure of the screenplay which was eventually shot was not simply to trim down Towne's rambling first draft to eliminate extraneous characters and complicating sub-plots and incidents but to supply the story with a rigorous single perspective: that of the protagonist, J. J. Gittes. We discover as Jake discovers, we are never lagging behind him, we are never way ahead of him.

Apart, that is, for these few telling moments.

. . . .

We do not yet know who this woman is but we do know, along with Walsh and Duffy, that her presence is significant and troubling. For the duration of this shot we long to call out: 'Look out, she's behind you!' As soon as Jake does turn to see the woman who has witnessed his performance (a performance which we know from his banishment of Sophie is one which is normally denied to women) the conjunction of perspective is re-asserted: we discover as Jake discovers that this is the *real* Evelyn Mulwray.

The simple problematic which inaugurated the first act is abandoned and Jake's quest is transformed. His task now is to find out who set him up to spy on Mulwray, not only to extricate himself from the jeopardy he is in because of Mrs Mulwray's threatened law-suit, but to reassert his standing in his profession and recover his own *amour propre*. He is on the edge of a destabilising adventure, but he has, as yet, no desire to go any further. Jake's first reaction is to suppose that his task now is to get himself back to the position he was in at the start of the story, one of confidence and control, to go back to his initial status, not yet to go forward into potential chaos. So, when he returns to the Department of Water and Power to bluff his way into Mulwray's office, he tells the secretary: 'It's a personal matter.'

This minor character is one of many doorkeepers, a Threshold Guardian who will attempt to impede the hero's progress.[31] At this stage of the game, she is one who poses very little threat as Jake draws upon his resourcefulness simply by lying his way through the door in order to engage in what he thinks he does best: snooping. The first thing he sees is a photograph of Evelyn posing with a powerful stallion. Then a more serious impediment arrives in the shape of Mulwray's deputy, Yelburton. Though Jake has found certain clues in Mulwray's inner sanctum which propel him towards the enigma of water, he seems to discover nothing which helps in his quest to find out the identity of the girl. Yelburton deflects any such inquiries: Mulwray never even kids about an affair. 'Maybe', is Jake's rejoinder, 'he takes it very seriously.' He is speaking the truth without realising it and, in Yelburton's office, he is presented with another clue to the ultimate solution of the mystery, which he cannot as yet decipher, in the shape of the huge, stuffed fish on the wall.

3 6   A shape-shifter confronts a threshold guardian

As Jake is politely fobbed off he runs into Claude Mulvihill, visually defined as a classic heavy. In his thumb-nail sketch of this ape as illiterate and venal, Jake reveals for the first time, off-handedly, a past before the time span of this story – expressed, beautifully, through yet another elaboration of the water symbolism which drenches not only the tale but its telling: 'When Mulvihill here was Sheriff of Ventura County the rum-runners landed hundreds of tons on the beach and never lost a drop. He ought to be able to hold on to your water for you.' The fact that this dishonest former cop is now working for the department, ostensibly because of threats from the farmers in the valley to blow up the reservoir which holds the city's supply, not only compounds the suspicion of political corruption at the heart of the mystery but also provides the possibility of a direct physical threat to the protagonist.

So the seeds of future scenes are sown; set-ups are ready to be paid off.

Jake drives to the Mulwray place (one of the pleasures of this film is its use of L.A. architecture; this is one of those houses where, in Dick Powell/Philip Marlowe's words in *Murder, My Sweet/Farewell, My Lovely*, 'you need a compass to find the mail-box') to be confronted by another gatekeeper, the oriental butler. He literally closes the door in Jake's face before opening it again to allow him entrance. It is the function of such characters to either hinder or allow the hero's progress; here the butler does both. Jake is confronted by a panoply of Asian servants: a chauffeur, a maid and a gardener – this entire residence is a mini-Chinatown. He is told by the latter, as he drags weeds from the pond, that the water is bad for the grass. In parodying the gardener's

The rockpool – where life began. 'Velly bad for glass'

accent – 'velly bad for the glass' – Gittes is nearer to the truth than he can realise. He spots something in the pond, a clue which could lead to the solution of the entire mystery right now. Once again the detective is seeing without seeing, he doesn't get what is right before his eyes. For before he can fish out this mystery object, Evelyn appears in riding gear, looking hot and flushed from bare-back riding, a state which cannot but hint at a wild sexuality beneath this respectable surface.

At several points within this scene the film could end: Jake could accept Mrs Mulwray's sudden and surprising offer to 'drop the whole thing' and, more significantly, Evelyn could tell him what she knows about 'that little girlfriend' – but if either option were to happen there would be no more story. As in the schema perhaps most prominently at work in the novels of Dashiell Hammett, there is only a mystery because other characters will not tell the investigator the truth. It is Evelyn who wants not to proceed; she tells Jake that her husband seems to think he is an innocent man – 'I've been accused of a lot of things before but never that' – and Jake who resists. He keeps the story going not, as we have seen, in order to go forward but in order to go back to his standing before both Mrs Mulwrays – real and phoney – entered his office, before he had become a 'local joke', before he was 'caught with his pants down' – a state of undress he is accustomed to seeing only in others. He can't drop the case – not because he cares about the Mulwrays, nor because he has a financial and contractual obligation, but because of his own sense of self. This will put him in direct physical danger. So Evelyn supplies him with the next point in his quest for Mulwray: the Oak Hill reservoir and, for another brief moment, we are allowed a glimpse denied our hero: the sight of Evelyn's enigmatic (we might almost say 'inscrutable') face.

Another location, another threshold guardian, but this one is more formidable and a deeper plunge into the detective's reservoir of resources is needed to get past this barrier. Here we see a perfect instance of the 'set-up/pay-off' routine. Jake needs to get into a place in which he is not allowed, he needs a lucky charm. Only by claiming to be someone he is not, by shape-shifting, by disguise, can he effect that entrance. His only 'open sesame' is a way of pretending to be someone officially allowed to be there, someone from the department. So Towne has cleverly, at the time almost subliminally, inserted into the scene in Yelburton's office a plausible request for one of his cards, setting up a

situation which is paid off here as Jake produces the card and stylishly and easily effects an entrance without the need for any physical effort.

And it is here that Jake meets a character who is marked as being significant in both his past in the backstory and in his future in the progression of the story. Lieutenant Lou Escobar, a detective of Hispanic descent, clearly knows Jake well but his feelings about him are ambiguous. He cannot hide his envy when complimenting him on his clothes.[32] He allows Jake to smoke in a place where it's not normally allowed but seems to take a malicious delight in the thought of Jake getting his 'fingers burnt'. And, as Jake puts him down: 'Still putting Chinamen in jail for spitting in the laundry?', Lou lets Jake know he's out of date. 'I'm out of Chinatown now' – a remark which, we will eventually learn, cannot be applied to Jake himself.

For the first time there is a hint of what 'Chinatown' means. Once again, Towne's assurance that the audience shares Jake's point of view is revealed as a species of dissemblance. For what we do not share is the knowledge of Jake's past; he has not yet chosen to reveal it, he is choosing to deny it to himself. We know less, at this point, than the protagonist. But we may already suspect that 'Chinatown' is more than

Polanski's 'real-life' location, more even than Towne's 'state of mind', it is the ultimate organising principle of the story.

. . . .

Chinatown is a detective story and, at heart, this is an optimistic genre with a touching faith in the eventual victory of human rationality. The pact that the writer makes with the audience, the reader or the viewer, is that at the start of the story we do not know the perpetrator of the crime but we know that by the conclusion our surrogate, the investigator, will have found out on our behalf. So this story form necessarily presupposes the excavation and display of things which, at the start of the tale, remain deliberately hidden from view. It is the role of the detective to return the repressed back into the light of societal scrutiny.

Also, as has often been said, the detective story is not one tale but two: it is the story of a crime and the story of the solution of that crime. So such tales must always, therefore, presuppose a double time frame. The investigator must re-evoke, reconstruct and remember events which took place before the time that the investigation was initiated. Every individual detective story must negotiate a particular narrative path through both the time it takes the protagonist (the detective) to move from an initial lack of information to an eventual full possession of the facts from the time which preceded the investigation, the time when the crime took place.[33] This temporal doubling will always pose a story-telling problem, which every screenplay writer is forced to solve, as plots are characterised by a relentlessly forward-flowing cause-and-effect narrative thrust, but dependent on events which took place before the tale began. Be that as it may, the central narrative dynamic of every detective story is the movement from lack of knowledge to possession of knowledge – what we might call the gnostic imperative.

As Vladimir Propp, the initiator of modern structural analysis of popular narrative, suggested, all stories must start with the central character (or, indeed, characters) being defined as having something missing,[34] whether they know it or not, and it is that which propels them on their narrative journey, their quest. In other words, all stories are predicated on a lack. Every specific story genre tends to depend on particular founding lacks that will be overcome by the eventual closure.

So in a love story the object of the quest is usually a person and the protagonist's pursuit is not only to discover but, ultimately, to have and to hold the object of his or her love, to surmount the obstacles that society or the loved one's family put in the path of fulfilment. In the adventure story the quest is more often for a physical object, the Lost Ark of the Covenant, the Topkapi jewels, something that the hero needs to possess. It is evident that the central quest of the protagonist in a detective story is for knowledge. In *Chinatown*, J. J. Gittes has to find out something that at the beginning of the story he is not even aware that he doesn't know and, as in most sophisticated tales of whatever generic stamp, he will come to realise that the knowledge does not pertain just to the outside world, but also to his own self.

In thus defining the detective story as a species of gnostic initiation on the part of the investigator as acolyte, it can be seen that this journey – from the darkness of ignorance to the light of knowledge – must also necessarily involve a transformation on the part of the person who undertakes it. Every protagonist in every story must go on a journey. He (it is a 'he' in this particular tale) must end up in a different place, physical and/or psychological, from the one in which he started. So, the structure of the story in general, and of the detective story in this instance, can be seen to be analogous to the ritual process that anthropologists have labelled the *rite de passage*.

The Rite of Passage describes the ritual movement, through a social process, of an individual from one status in the community to another.[35] The pertinence of a model of such a ritual is by no means confined to those films which openly proclaim themselves as tales of defining events in the life cycles of, for instance and not infrequently, adolescent males. I would go much further and suggest that *all* stories must reflect the deep structure of the Rites of Passage.

In such rites, then, individuals move from one socially prescribed status to another: from childhood to adulthood, from boy to warrior, from girl to woman, from single to married – the terms will be radically different in every society whilst the structural movement will be essentially the same. Having attained a new social status, the individual is recognised by the whole of society as having a different set of rights and responsibilities. A girl can leave her mother's village to live in the house of her in-laws only after marriage. A boy can travel away from the social group to pursue the path of his ancestors only after initiatory circumcision. Every society defines and copes with these life changes in idiosyncratic ways, but all communities, even such a ritually impoverished society such as our own, seem to feel the need to mark them.

Even when the change of state is apparently straightforwardly physiological, as, it would seem, the movement from being alive to being dead, it cannot be accepted by a social group as having taken place unless and until the appropriate funerary ceremony has been performed.

These rituals are a necessary attempt by our species to structure the meaninglessness of mere physical time, the inevitability of mere biological growth and decay. They have the effect of proclaiming the supremacy of culture over nature, of mind over matter. But any change in social status is a risky business, it cannot simply be asserted. It leaves a hole in the status that has been left and another space needs to be created in the status to be attained. As in drama (deriving from a Greek word which means 'action') progress can only take place in ritual through a terrain of conflict. So these transformatory journeys must, naturally, be full of tension.

For a time, the protagonists of such rites have abandoned the state they once felt comfortable occupying but have not yet arrived at the state they've set out for. Separated from one state, they are yet to be incorporated into another. So, for a while, they become as unrecognisable, uncategorisable and unstable as the never-never land they temporarily occupy.

The anthropologist Arnold van Gennep, working at the turn of the century, called this structural space *la marge* – the margins – but I prefer to opt for a more cinematic denomination. I like to call it 'The Liminal Zone', vamping van Gennep's disciple, Victor Turner.[36] You are no longer in control of either the vertical or the horizontal hold. You are in this physical and temporal in-between limbo space and the normal patterns of social behaviour and authority are no longer operative. Following the regular road map seems only to make matters worse. The only place to stay is in the Bates Motel, every channel on the TV is showing *The Outer Limits* and the only place to eat is in Chinatown.

This in-between space in the journey from status *a* to status *b*, when the participant is neither *a* nor *b* is not just the space of Ritual, but the space of Story. I would go further to assert that, for the audience as well as for the writer (who must also go on a journey of creation, starting with nothing, moving through the chaos of creation, ending, it is to be hoped, with something beautiful, meaningful) story-telling is often the nearest we come, in our secularised society, to any kind of ritual experience. I am, of course, using 'ritual' throughout not in the everyday sense as worn-out, repetitive behaviour drained of meaning but as a dynamic structural model of individual change within a social framework.

So in *Chinatown* it is not so much the topographical area of the title as the very memory of that space where nobody knows anything which becomes the metaphor for the Liminal Zone Jake Gittes must enter and traverse on our behalf if he is to solve the double enigma at the heart of the tale.

Which is a roundabout way of saying that 'Chinatown' is, in fact, a perfect title for a complex detective thriller with dimensions which are political (about the nature of power), sexual (about the nature of gender), metaphysical (about the nature of evil), psychological (about the nature of the self) and philosophical (about the nature of knowledge).

. . . .

Clearly these two men, Lou and Jake – one still an insider in the Police Department – share a history which will be revealed, but whether Escobar is on Jake's side is still open to doubt. But the plot is advanced when Escobar tells him that once again he is too late – this time to talk to Hollis Mulwray. For, right at this moment, the commissioner's body is being hurled from the run-off channel. His bow-tie is twisted, he is without his glasses, one shoe is missing and his face is grotesquely set – all in all he looks like a fugitive from one of Polanski's early absurdist shorts, *Two Men and a Wardrobe* (1958) perhaps.

The prelude of the next scene, in which Escobar quizzes Evelyn about her husband's 'alleged affair', hinting that Mulwray's death may not have been accidental but suicide brought on by the publicity, is the first and only dialogue scene played without the presence of Jake (although we might assume he is outside the office, ear-wigging). Evelyn stutters when asked about the identity and whereabouts of 'the young lady in question' and contradicts herself when trying to maintain the subterfuge that she hired Gittes to find out about a liaison which 'came as a complete surprise' to her. Then Jake enters the scene, rescuing her from the lawman and protecting her from the press men who try to photograph her as she struggles to put on dark glasses. He poses for the cameras, anything but publicity-shy, but is surprised when she offers to send him a cheque: 'to make it official that I've hired you'.

This is what is known in the trade as a 'plot-point', a moment in which the terms and conditions of the tale suddenly shift around and the premise of the next act is inaugurated. It is obvious that this will centre around the relationship between Jake and Evelyn and that the enigma will reside within her and not within a reservoir. But there is still, to paraphrase Sam Goldwyn, a lot of water to be passed.[37]

Jake goes to the morgue to see Mulwray's body and meets Morty, the aptly named morgue attendant – a large, chain-smoking, jovial and welcoming door-opener who looks and sounds like he came straight from central casting in the 40s: 'Middle of a drought and the water commissioner drowns. Only in L.A.' And it is here that, apparently co-incidentally, Jake finds out about a drunk who had been living in a storm drain of the dried-up river. He too has drowned. The scene sows the seed for the one that follows.

A return to a previous location: the spot where Jake had first watched Mulwray. Menacing music accompanies his descent to the river bed and there he finds the little Mexican boy who had been talking with Mulwray – a minor character reprised to give vital information to the investigator. By now we are coming to the same conclusions as Jake: someone must be manipulating the water supply, presumably somehow to ensure that the plan to build the reservoir goes through. So the obvious place for Jake to go is back to the reservoir where Mulwray's body was found. By now it is night. The obstacle to entrance is now only the physical gate and, ignoring the 'Keep Out' sign, he simply climbs over. Then two shots are heard, evidently a signal to open the sluice, the literal 'water gate', as a torrent comes racing down, carrying Jake with it and slamming him against the barrier.

'This guy's got water on the brain'

As an aside, it is obvious that this dangerous stunt was performed by the star himself. As Polanski tells it:

> I wanted to do this in a single shot, with Jack's face clearly visible and coming into close-up as he hit the wire mesh barrier across the channel, so there was no possibility of using his stunt man ... We saved the dam scene till the very end – in case something happened ... Knowing that it would take four hours to prepare the set again after a full rehearsal, I sweet-talked Jack into doing the take without one. Like a true pro he agreed.[38]

And as Jake walks away, the film cannot resist a telling little rhyme (which conveys the possibility that Mulwray must also have met his end in this manner), for Gittes, like Mulwray, is also devoid of one item of footwear: 'Son of a bitch! Goddam Florsheim shoe.'

But Jake is not yet out of physical jeopardy as he is approached by a dapper little man in a white suit, spotted red bow-tie and a Panama, a character credited as 'the man with the knife', a character played by the director of *Knife in the Water*, the director of *Chinatown*, a character described by Gittes as 'the midget', who is flanked by Mulvihill in an image resonant of *Le Gros et Le Maigre* (Polanski, 1961). Towne says this incident of 'nasal violence' was irresistible to impose upon a detective, someone who is always poking his nose into other people's business ('a very nosy fellow') and irresistible also, presumably, as a phallic displacement for a character ultimately revealed to be impotent. Even here, another water reference also proves irresistible; next time, the Midget threatens, he'll 'cut it off and feed it to my goldfishes'. But Towne also makes the point that this incident 'informs the potential for violence' in the story. Even though there is surprisingly little Kensington Gore employed in the rest of the film, as Polanski says: '[a]s usual, I conveyed more violence than was actually seen'.[39]

Back in his office, in daylight and in a place of safety, we are permitted to witness Walsh's reaction before we can relish the great white beacon of a bandage which now dominates Jake's face. Both Towne and Polanski want to take credit for insisting that the detective's wound would not make a miraculous movie overnight recovery. Whoever had the idea, it was by displaying the various bandages which cover the proboscis, whilst – like displaced cod-pieces – continually drawing attention towards it, the consequences of an act of violence remain out on parade.

His associates, too, try to talk Jake out of pursuing the incident: whoever's responsible for this is liable to be politically well-connected. But the possibility of dropping the case is once again removed as the outside enters their world in the form of a phone call from Ida Sessions, 'the one who pretended to be Mrs Mulwray'. As is usual for such an informant, she tantalisingly withholds as well as gives over information. She refuses to say who employed her, which would, of course, solve the enigma. But she propels the action forward from its temporary stasis by revealing that if he looks in the obituary column of the paper he can find 'one of those people'.

As Gittes waits in a restaurant (now with a slightly smaller nasal appendage) he tears out the list of as yet meaningless names from a newspaper which provides the double service of revealing, in a front page headline, that the Water Bond Issue has been passed. Then Evelyn enters, in widow's weeds, also concerned to pay him off and stop the story. He catalogues her contradictory actions and accuses her of hiding something. He is, of course, entirely correct, but not in the terms of the political conspiracy he has in mind. He thinks Mulwray's death was neither accidental nor suicidal, but murder, because he had stumbled upon the plot to dump the water, a plot which is being covered up at the highest level.

Eventually Evelyn concurs: she has been holding out on him, she knew about the affair but was grateful for it; an explanation that 'runs contrary to [Jake's] experience' as someone whose *métier* is 'matrimonial work', unless it was because it allowed her to conduct her own affairs (the scenario of the Chinaman joke). When asked where she was at the time of her husband's death she answers that she can't tell him, from which he concludes she 'was seeing someone too'. But when pressed if this had been going on for very long she neurotically answers: 'I don't see anyone for very long, Mr Gittes. It's difficult for me.'

No lies are told, but no truths are revealed. The precise wording of her enigmatic answers needs to be filtered through a lens Jake does not yet possess. But he does find out one other piece of information: that the 'C' on her personalised stationery stands for 'Cross', her maiden name. Jake seems evidently perplexed when his revelation of her husband's murder seems to be treated so lightly: 'It seems like half the city is trying to cover it up, which is fine by me. But I goddamn near lost my nose and I like it. I like breathing through it … and I still think you're hiding something.' The squeal of his tyres as his car races away hides her cracked appeal to him, which we see but he doesn't. Now we are momentarily ahead of him, we are sure she possesses the answer to the riddle.

. . . .

It is necessary now for the detective to retrace his steps, to return to another location he has already visited, to try and see what he missed before. Back in the Water Department this time he sees a photo of the man his operative snapped arguing with Jake's original quarry and he notices his name: Noah Cross. Noah, the name of that Biblical patriarch most associated with excess of water rather than with, as in this city, drought, and Cross, an instrument of torture, a symbol of redemption … well, Evelyn's maiden name at least.[40] The frosty monosyllabic secretary is, on this occasion, not so easily duped although she does unknowingly impart vital information: that Cross was Mulwray's partner, that they once *owned* the city's water supply. This time around Jake has to irritate her into letting him cross her threshold, by smoking, by tapping his cigarette, by humming, by whistling.

Another piece of subtle sound design (complex throughout the film) provides a ground bass to his wait: a scraping noise proves to be Mulwray's name literally rubbed out from the door of the department. Within Yelburton's inner sanctum Jake reveals what he knows thus far – explaining how the bad guys will know what he knows. Yelburton fobs him off with an explanation which will need to be verified: the water is being diverted to help the farmers in the valley, outside the city limits. So in this scene crucial information which informs the historical background to the tale is efficiently given as well as setting up two further ports of call for Jake.

Jake's progress is halted by the presence of Evelyn in his office. She's still dressed in black, she's still jumpy. Now she wishes to hire him officially – to find Hollis's murderer. Her nervousness is accentuated when Jake mentions Noah Cross, confirmed as her father – a word she stutters out and stumbles over, lighting a cigarette when she already has one going; all her neurotic Freudian ticks are stimulated by this word. Her explanation for this is simple, probably true, definitely partial: her father and her husband quarrelled over the latter's desire that the water should belong to the public. She says they fell out long ago, but Jake already knows that the two men were seen together at the beginning of the tale.

So it is no surprise that Jake's next step, at almost the mid-point of the film, is to beard the villain in his lair.

John Huston, a Hollywood patriarch with a devilish reputation, incarnates the Father. His domain is not a cave deep underground nor in the middle of a dense forest, but he is a mythological figure nonetheless. In fact he can be found at a pleasant, well-appointed location, naturally by the sea – at the Albacore Club (do those syllables strike a chord?) – a potentate whose symbol is a fish. Can we not but be reminded of the Fisher King – a tainted ruler presiding over a barren waste land?[41]

Cross leans on a walking stick, like that three-legged creature that walks in the evening in the Sphinx's riddle. He displays his superiority (wilfully mispronouncing 'Gittes' as 'Gits' in spite of constant correction); his untouchable venerability ('[p]oliticians, ugly buildings and whores all get respectable if they last long enough') and his corrupting hospitality as he serves Jake an unsettling fish with its head still on and whose eye looks up at Jake with a dead, unseeing stare. This is a fish, like the investigator in this scene, out of water. A long spoon is necessary when supping with this man. Cross is entirely beyond the normal protocols of social interaction.

Though Cross accuses Jake of taking his daughter 'for a ride' his toothy, simian grin doesn't crack for a moment when he asks, with lascivious fascination, if he is 'sleeping with her'.[42] In pumping 'Gits' about the police investigation the backstory expositional information emerges smoothly that Escobar (an honest man who, nevertheless, 'has to swim in the same water we all do') was, indeed, Jake's partner in Chinatown. When Cross cautions him about Evelyn: 'You may think you know what you're dealing with but, believe me, you don't,' Jake responds by saying: 'That's what the District Attorney used to tell me in Chinatown.' At last, face-to-face with the ultimate villain of the piece, the metaphor of the title is made explicit: Chinatown as a place where secure knowledge is impossible and Chinatown as a symbol for the feminine enigma. '*Cherchez*', as Evelyn will later say, '*la femme.*'

Which is precisely what Cross wants Gittes to do: find the other woman, offering Jake a return to his original (bogus) assignment. The only time Jake unsettles Cross is when he reveals that he knows he recently met Mulwray (we see Cross's reaction; Jake doesn't, he doesn't have to). When asked what the argument was about, Cross answers: 'My daughter.' When pressed he says only: 'Just find the girl.' In Proppian terms it is one of the functions of the *villain* to 'disturb the peace of a happy family, to cause some form of misfortune, damage, or harm'.[43] You can say that again. If the connection between these two statements of Cross could be brought into the light then, once again, there would be no more story. But Jake has to suffer plenty more yet. Cross's apparent anxiety at what the 'very jealous' Evelyn 'might do to her' sows the seeds that Evelyn is a threat, that somehow *she* is the black widow who lurks at the centre of the web.

Jake now goes via the Hall of Records to check on the ownership of land in the valley where, according to Yelburton, water is being diverted. The weasly, fastidious gate-keeper here is no match for Gittes's wiles. Ascertaining that so many names have been recently pasted onto deed titles, indicating that vast tracts of land have recently changed hands, he simply coughs loudly as he rips the evidence from the records (using an instrument, the ruler, unknowingly supplied by the gate-keeper himself).

Although the pleasure of this moment lies in witnessing our hero triumph over the petty obstacles placed in his path towards knowledge, nevertheless there is a visual rhyme here with a prior instance of Jake ripping out a list of names.

The next sequence, the confrontation with the farmers in the orange grove in the valley, was, due to the complex exigencies of scheduling, the first to be shot as the owner of the land wanted the crew out before it was time to harvest his oranges.[44] Polanski had disagreed from the start about the look of the film with Evans who had, apparently, suggested warm, saturated tones like those Gordon Willis (who wasn't available) had achieved for Evans's success, *The Godfather*. 'I saw *Chinatown* not as a "retro" piece or conscious imitation of classic movies shot in black and white, but as a film about the thirties seen through the camera eye of the seventies.'[45] Though he insisted on his designer, Richard Sylbert, and his costumier, Anthea Sylbert (Richard's sister-in-law), conveying 'a scrupulously accurate reconstruction of décor, costume and idiom', Polanski wanted to avoid a nostalgic parody of 1930s film techniques.[46]

Nevertheless, Polanski did want 'a cameraman who could identify with the period'[47] and settled on one of the old masters of chiaroscuro,

Stanley Cortez, who had been working in American pictures since 1937, coincidentally the year the film was set, and had shot (amongst many other brilliant pictures) *Night of the Hunter* for Charles Laughton in 1955 and, singled out by Polanski as a 'splendid evocation of a vanished period', Welles's *The Magnificent Ambersons* in 1942.

Polanski, though, was less than satisfied with the first week's rushes: '[e]verything was coming out in shades of ochre and tomato ketchup'.[48] Although he soon discovered that this was because of Evans's instructions to the lab, he still felt that the choice of the veteran cameraman, though 'full of old-fashioned charm', had been a mistake:

> Completely out of touch with mainstream developments in the technology of film-making, he began asking for equipment that was no longer in use ... He used an inordinate amount of light and was so excruciatingly slow that, had we kept him on, we would never have finished the picture.[49]

He was, of course, a cinematographer who had come late in life to colour photography and perhaps was also unaccustomed to composing for the Panavision anamorphic format. One might also speculate that beginning what was predominantly a studio picture (more than two-thirds of the film was shot at Paramount) with a dusty sequence was not conducive to his way of working. So ten days into the shoot Polanski had to fire him, replacing him with John A. Alonzo.

Alonzo later wrote a short article about his approach[50] in which he states that he 'studiously avoided gimmicks', dispensing, for instance, with any lens diffusion when shooting the female star. He stuck, by and large, to lenses of a focal length between *f*.2.8 and *f*.4 to give the film what he calls a 'classic', entirely untricksy, look which doesn't draw attention to itself in any expressionistic manner (unlike, of course, many of the also 'classic' film noirs) and which, I would add, perfectly complements the classical construction of the screenplay. Interestingly enough, though, Alonzo specifically cites the influence of two cameramen associated with the period in which Cortez was flourishing: James Wong Howe and Gregg Toland, both pioneers of deep focus cinematography in black and white.

All of this technical practicality only serves to demonstrate, if it shows nothing else, how wrong the theorists can be. Fredric Jameson, in an otherwise timely intervention upon and definition of the contours of the 'post-modern' world[51] (a concept which already, at this time of writing, seems so much a thing of the past), characterises *Chinatown* as a 'stylistic recuperation of the American ... 1930s', seeing the film as an attempt 'to lay siege either to our own present and immediate past, or to a more distant history that escapes individual existential memory'.

Though this film can evidently be seen as very definitely a product of its time, its predominant concerns cannot be simply reduced to those of a phoney reflection of the past. Only think of how it avoids all the pitfalls of a retrospective soundtrack. If there is an argument to be had with *Chinatown* it will not be because of its knowing evocation of the past, but rather with its romantic anxiety about the present. The ultimate problem of this film for me lies not in the complicit wink of the post-modern but the unblinking stare of the classical.

....

An interdiction only exists in a tale so that it can be violated, so Jake's car drives past the warning signs propelling himself into escalating physical jeopardy. From this point on he will be, on more than occasion, lucky to escape with his life. The first threat comes from these 'dumb Oakies', recent rural immigrants to the Promised Land of California, presumably having been forced out of their homes by a banker such as the one in the barber shop.[52] The detective, urban and urbane, is out of his milieu among the orange groves and, in the film's only chase sequence, is no match for his pursuers even though they are mounted on horseback. Unsurprisingly, his car overheats and, in another rhyme, steam pours out of the radiator. Before he is knocked out he learns that, far from being surreptitiously aided by Yelburton, the Water Department have been poisoning their wells and blowing up their water tanks in an attempt to drive them from their land.

When he comes to, it is Evelyn's face he sees; she has been summoned by the farmer who found her name in his wallet – a search which has served the double function to establish that Jake isn't carrying a gun. Now she can function as a means to get him out of this situation. For the first time, and only temporarily, she operates as his partner and as his sounding board – his Watson – to hear his (now almost complete) theory of the political chicanery surrounding the murder of her husband. The dam is 'a con job', the people of the city are being tricked into paying for a water supply which has provided the impetus for the land grab of this arid territory through which they drive at twilight. All Jake now needs to confirm is who is behind the conspiracy. As he recites an inventory of names of the new owners of this now worthless land which will one day soon be so valuable we might be alert enough to recognise one bizarre appellation, particularly as it is singled out by Evelyn: Jasper Lamar Crabb, one of the names from the obit. column. The land is being bought in the names of dead people.

The logic of the tale now takes them both to the Mar Vista Rest Home, Crabb's last abode. Once again Jake plays the shape-shifter, worming his way past yet another intransigent gate-keeper in the guise of, appropriately enough, a member of a dysfunctional family: a son who has fallen out with his father. The joy of performance in this scene lies in seeing the detective as master of disguise (although, unlike Sherlock Holmes, he doesn't even alter his appearance), Jake's recovery of his knowing smirk and in watching the two stars working so well together, a partnership with a common goal. Evelyn even looks at Jake with admiration at his resourcefulness as he turns every setback to his own advantage in his attempts to find out the names of the inhabitants.

> *Jake*: Do you accept people of the Jewish persuasion?
> *Director*: I'm afraid …
> *Jake*: That's all right, neither does Dad.

This interchange exposes en route the segregated nature of Los Angeles society in the 30s. Thus an aspect of the societal background is revealed through a seemingly less than significant piece of character business. When they do get inside, even this old folks' home is partially characterised through non-sanctioned sexuality, as a nurse rebukes one of the old men for goosing her.

Here they see, on the activities board, a list of the owners of a '50,000 acre empire', and here, at the centre of a quilt being sewn by these senescent, unwitting proprietors, they see the crest of the Albacore Club owner (not 'applecore', as Walsh originally thought, 'it's a fish'): Noah Cross, charitable patron of the Mar Vista. Now Jake thinks he sees everything, that all the pieces are in place and he also thinks he has an ally, although she doesn't yet know that he knows about her father's involvement. But he is rumbled by the suspicious threshold guardian who has called in reinforcements. Jake, weaponless it has been established, has to resort to physical violence to escape from Mulvihill, the Midget and a third party (who looks very like the unspeaking heavy who was at Cross's marina) who shoots at them after Jake is again rescued by Evelyn in her new role as sidekick, saving his 'ass … neck'.

So the terms and conditions for a closer liaison have been set. But liminality is not far away as he confides in her that he hasn't been involved in such direct physical violence since his days in Chinatown.

> *Evelyn*: What were you doing there?
> *Jake*: Working for the District Attorney.
> *Evelyn*: Doing what?
> *Jake*: As little as possible.
> *Evelyn*: The District Attorney gives his men advice like that?
> *Jake*: They do in Chinatown.
> *Evelyn*: Why did you leave the police force?

He dodges the 'innocent question', deflecting attention to his injury, prefiguring that this topic is, for him, the site of unresolved inner conflict.

Evelyn saves Jake's ass … neck

So in Evelyn's home, at night, his bandage is finally removed, his naked wound exposed, although, from now on, his ability to sniff out the right scent will not be markedly improved. And as Evelyn treats him she also reveals an imperfection of her own, something black in the green part of her eye, a f-f-flaw – a word she stumbles over like f-f-father, her own site of unresolved trauma – a 'birthmark', a sign of tainted blood, a sign of imperfect vision. A bloodied nose and a defective eye come together in a screen kiss.

It was Polanski, apparently, who demanded that Jake and Evelyn should go to bed together, but the scene is anything but gratuitous, shoe-horned in out of a male director's commercially motivated voyeuristic whim. As soon as the camera tracks past the post-coital cigarette up Jake's arm to rest on a beautifully composed static set-up which positions them both on either side of the Panavision frame, in naked alliance, we cannot help but realise how little we know about these characters' sexualities. Evelyn was initially presented flushed from riding bare-back and had hinted strongly at serial short-term affairs, but we suspect that this was mere flim-flam to put the detective off the scent with a confession of the type of lust with which his 'matrimonial work' has made him only too familiar. Jake's libidinous drive seemed at first only for social status, 'an honest living', though this has been transformed into a lust for knowledge. He has not yet spoken of past affairs – perhaps he has been sufficiently satisfied by the professional, quotidian keyhole-peeping, or perhaps he has been sated, even disgusted, by it.

A bloodied nose and a defective eye come together

We are denied a concomitant voyeuristic pleasure as their moments of togetherness take place in between the cut from the kiss to the smouldering cigarette end, conventional cinematic framing devices of the sexual act. When Evelyn, smiling, possessed with a calmness we have not been privy to before, does finally speak it is to take up the dangling conversation and so evoke a past he wishes to, if not forget, at least put out of his mind: 'Did you wear a uniform?' 'Gimme a break, will you?' He is instantly transported back to Chinatown where, 'You can't always tell what's going on. Like with you.' And finally she gets it out of him: 'I was trying to keep someone from being hurt. I ended up making sure she *was* hurt.'

'Chinatown' is revealed not just as a place in the past where no one knew what was going on, where it's best to do nothing but, much more dynamically, as a metaphorical site still mentally present where, if you do attempt to act, action will result in tragic, unforeseen consequences. So now the dominant theme which organises the rest of the film is uncovered: what Towne calls 'the futility of good intentions'.[53] In Chinatown it is better not to act, much better not to know. We are learning along with Evelyn something that the protagonist had not yet revealed to us – something in his backstory which casts a determining shadow over his present.

But this is all Evelyn is allowed to learn as *her* present now floods in with a phone call which 'has nothing to do with any of this'. Their intimacy is finally completely shattered when he reveals he has already seen Noah Cross. She pulls away, the evocation of the Father as the ultimate passion-killer. Echoing Cross's description of his daughter as 'disturbed' she now calls her father 'dangerous' and 'crazy'.

Though she begs Jake to trust her, it is evident he does not. He kicks one of the tail-lights out of her car, functionally so that he can follow her through night-time traffic, re-evoking the kind of detective methodology which was so much a part of the texture of the film when it started as an apparently straightforward investigative yarn but, more significantly, to inaugurate a metaphorical chain which will permeate the rest of the film and lead inexorably to the literal streets of Chinatown whose ethos is now prefigured by a disharmonious oriental musical theme.

Evelyn, unsettled once again, is let into a modest house by her butler, providing an answer to Jake's 'innocent question' as to why there were no servants in the Mulwray home. Peeping in, he sees but does not get the whole picture: Hollis's girlfriend is on a bed, evidently held against her will by Evelyn who seems to be forcibly feeding her medication. When Jake confronts Evelyn her head falls forward in anguish, momentarily knocking against the horn of her car. Jake threatens to call the police but Evelyn tells him that the 'other woman' is, in fact, her sister, distressed at having just learned of Mulwray's death. Refusing her offer to come home with her Jake says, 'I'm tired, Mrs Mulwray'. It seems as if all the narrative strands are weaving together to expose Evelyn, in spite of her protestations that she would never have hurt her husband, as the classic (indeed, stereotypical) frozen-hearted, castrating film noir heroine – *trouvez la femme fatale*: 'noted for changeability and treachery … In the noir thriller, where the male … is not in control of the plot, not only is the hero frequently not sure whether the woman is honest or a deceiver, but the heroine's characterisation is itself fractured …'[54] Evelyn is abandoned, her face half in light, half in darkness; unreadable, enigmatic.

. . . .

Film noir is not a genre like the Western or the gangster film, instantly defined by location or the presence of conventional characters. Neither is it, like the detective or the love story, defined by a particular pattern of narrative development – there are noir Westerns, gangsters, love stories and detective movies. It is not a classificatory term that originates from within the American film industry itself but from criticism, French criticism at that,[55] and one

'I was trying to keep someone from being hurt. I ended up making sure she *was* hurt'

whose definitional limits critics don't always seem to agree upon. The term usually designates a cycle of films with a common low-key visual style, 'anti-traditional' if not entirely antithetical to the bright, balanced studio look of the 30s;[56] a discordant, unstable *mise en scène*; a not infrequent complexity of temporal narration and a concomitant, if imprecisely defined, knowing, sardonic 'sensibility'. Small wonder we love it.

For many commentators, such as the screenwriter and director Paul Schrader,[57] the term can only be applied to films from a specific period of cinema history, roughly the middle 40s and early 50s, and is often associated with the work of emigré German directors and cinematographers with their roots in expressionism cinema, coupled with a home-grown mood of post-war disillusionment and cold war paranoia, evincing, he says, 'a passion for the past and the present, but also a fear of the future …' peopled with characters who are 'small-time, unredeemed, unheroic'.

By most of these criteria, then, a studio film made in 1974, deliberately shot in non-expressionistic 'classical' style in Panavision and Technicolor with an uncluttered narrative style entirely devoid of flashbacks or first-person voice-over narration could hardly, it would seem, be categorised as a 'modern film noir', even for those for whom this phrase would itself be a contradiction in terms. Nevertheless, it is understandable why certain critics have seen in *Chinatown* evidence that 'the film noir is not dead'.[58] There is something profoundly 'un-American' in the cynicism and despair which permeates the social vision of the film noir (if one definition of 'Americanism' is the Panglossian

The dark lady, the spider woman

boosterism of human mutability and social perfectibility in this best of all possible worlds – California, Here I Come!) and this mood is present in spades in the final act of this Polish exile's film.

It is perhaps, however, in the depiction of Evelyn Cross Mulwray where noir-ish shadows play most evidently and it is the figure of the woman in film noir which has been a particular focus of feminist film theory since the time *Chinatown* was produced. 'The dark lady, the spider woman, the evil seductress who tempts man and brings about his destruction'[59] is how the 'female archetype' of the film noir has been characterised and this is the image of the female lead which is now consciously evoked.

This is, however, a conventional portrayal of the woman of which the system of this film is entirely aware, which will be built up only to be undercut, not as an instance of 'post-modernist' nod-and-wink complicit knowingness but as yet another image in the paradigm of false images necessary to the story's most fundamental theme. It is an image Lou Escobar, the lawman, can hold entirely unproblematically but one which it is Jake's tragedy to be seduced into sharing and, to our shame, we will go along with it, for a while, without protestation. Evelyn does not speak not because she has been denied a voice but because she has deliberately chosen not to bring the past out into the open. She chooses not to tell what she knows not because she is repressing but because she knows too much to share Jake's blind faith in revelation. Although Jake will consider her a betrayer he will come to learn that it is she who has been betrayed, and not least by himself for thinking of her thus. Although she will be mortally unsuccessful in her (as yet unrevealed) mission it is not Evelyn who will be the film's ultimate victim, its patsy. That role is pre-ordained not for the heroine but for the hero.

. . . .

Jake's only recourse is to retreat to his home (a place we've never been allowed access into before), a temporary sanctuary, and there to take a shower, to engage in an act of ritual ablution, to try and sleep alone, to shut out the night. It is an instant of calm, showing a Jake we've not seen before: spent, no longer driven by a desire to know, to possess the facts. But this is a film and it cannot last. The phone rings, the outside world intrudes and an address is given for Ida Sessions, the stand-in of the woman he has just been relieved to leave; an address in Echo Park, where his snooping almost began.

It is early morning now; it is a scene used a thousand times before: the P.I. is to be led into a snare where the police will find him with a dead body (incidentally, when searching Ida's wallet he catches a glimpse of her membership card for the Screen Actors' Guild – she is a disposable body, a 'working woman'). Operating outside the law's authority Jake is nonetheless vulnerable to its jurisdiction; it's a frame-up. Escobar's partner, Loach, displays the sanctioned lawman's characteristic contempt for Jake's lucrative profession: 'What happened to your nose, Gittes, somebody slam a bedroom window on it?' But Jake is too quick for him, concretising the phallic symbolism of his wound: 'No, your wife got excited. She crossed her legs a little too quick. Understand what I mean, pal?'

The flatfoot takes the suggestion of cuckoldry (a return to the terrain of the Chinaman joke) personally – which was how it was meant. But in terms of what has just happened to Jake, who has only just left the bed of a dead man's wife, it is an image of the vagina as a sharp instrument, the woman as a lethal weapon, which resonates.

Now Lou thinks he knows everything: Sessions hired Jake, Jake followed Mulwray, Mulwray was murdered. He produces a vital piece of information, unknown to Jake: they found salt water in Mulwray's lungs. For Escobar this points inevitably to Evelyn as the murderer of her husband with Jake as his client's accessory after the fact, conspiring with her to hide the truth, perhaps even extorting from her to keep it quiet. Jake bristles at the charge of extortion: it's where he draws the line, a type of venality beyond the bounds of his albeit flexible moral code.

Two sides of the law

But he finds no problem with this new evidence: it only confirms his theory that the Water Commissioner was killed by the ocean where the water was being dumped. A return to this isolated spot does nothing to convince Escobar who seems ready to accept Yelburton's explanation. For Jake this is evidence of his former partner's tacit implication in the criminal activities of the powerful: he 'wants to hang on to his little gold bar'. Lou is now Jake's adversary who could 'take away his license'. Jake has to produce Evelyn.

Just as Jake takes out the tools of his trade to pick Evelyn's lock, the Chinese maid opens up – getting through doors is no longer a pertinent issue. The house is shut up, bags are packed. But the oriental gardener is still, as he needs to be, weeding around the pool: 'bad for glass'; but this time he glosses the statement: 'salt water … bad for glass.' If only he'd have said that before! Jake fishes out the evidence he had forgotten – in the pool are a pair of cracked spectacles, broken instruments of vision which both rhyme with the busted tail-light and are the smoking gun which will point to the identity of the murderer.

Suddenly it all becomes clear to Jake: Evelyn killed her husband in this domestic salt-water tide pool, forgetting to remove his glasses and now she plans to shut up the only witness, his young paramour, and flee having set Jake up as accessory. So Escobar's theory must be true: the feminine body is once again the site of chaotic transgression which threatens social stability. The policeman's patriarchal reading is seemingly confirmed and readily accepted. So Jake calls him, ready to turn his client in.

The obligatory scene, the scene everyone remembers, the scene often parodied, must now take place: Jake's showdown with the woman who has been variously his adversary, his employer, his lover and always the enigma, and who is now revealed as the culprit, the answer to the riddle. 'This is no time to be shocked by the truth', he tells her, but it is he who will be shocked as he displaces all the violence of the world of this story and all the frustration of his need to know into beating the truth out of her, 'Who is she?', all the time unaware that his desire for a straight answer blinds him, as he has always been blind, to the fact that Evelyn *is* telling the literal truth. The girl is her sister – he slaps her – her daughter – he slaps her – her sister – he slaps her – her daughter – he tosses her across the room, destabilising her as he struggles to regain his own stability – 'My sister AND my daughter!' This one simple connecting conjunction reveals a venal complexity beyond Jake's ken.

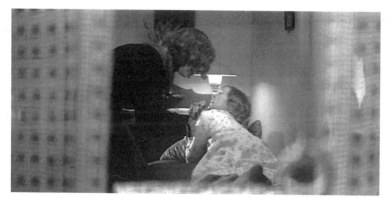

'My sister … my daughter … my sister AND my daughter'

So Jake sees correctly for the first time and, in seeing, realises that he is also implicated in the consequences of the crime. His hubristic zeal to solve the problem has only created another problem. His drive to bring a secret out into the open has led to the jeopardy of someone who only moments ago he thought of as the culprit and who is now revealed as the abused innocent party, an abuse which his actions have only compounded and intensified. He is coming to realise, as Towne himself put it, 'his own limits to act meaningfully'.

But there is still one piece of information outstanding: the glasses. And they couldn't have belonged to Hollis, 'he didn't wear bifocals'. So the tale has spun around again and the final act is inaugurated with another change in the protagonist's problematic. The question becomes no longer: 'who set me up?', 'what is the conspiracy?', 'who committed the murder?', but 'how can I save her?' It is Jake's task now to act, to free Evelyn from the danger he has put her into, to help her flee not only from her father but from the police by hiding her and her sister/daughter at the only place available: her butler's house on Alameda Street. He knows very well where that is: in Chinatown – that place where, we know only too well by now, his good intentions on a previous occasion led only to tragic consequences. And here she at last appears, 'the girl', now given a name (Katherine) as well as a body and a face which resembles that of Evelyn, but not, apart from saying 'hello' before immediately stepping back out of the frame, a voice.

Jake now no longer has to poke his nose in where it doesn't belong, nor sniff out the scent, rather he has to claw himself out of a hole of his own making. But, even though Escobar tells him that he'll 'never learn', he has not entirely exhausted all his wiles. By playing hard-to-get he forces the cop to make him go along, seemingly reluctantly, to the 'house in Pedro' where he has lied that Evelyn is hiding. How is he going to get out of this one? When he gets there the door is opened by a middle-aged matron we have seen before, but only from afar in compromising black and white photographs, the evidence of her illicit sexuality. For this is the house of Curly, his client from the very first scene – a scene which is now revealed as not only serving the purpose of illustrating Jake's grubby normality but also as a perfect set-up for this beautifully executed delayed pay-off. Curly, remember, was going to sell his van to pay Gittes's fee for revealing his wife's adultery; now Jake cashes in his debt by using the van as a means to effect his own escape and to ferry Evelyn and Katherine to freedom. Perhaps he's going to make it against all the odds. He assures Curly: 'Do you know how long I've been in this business?'

The complexity of the construction of this film, where every scene serves at least a double function and every move matters within its own symbolic system and narrative world!

But now Jake has to confront a danger far greater than that of the police: he has to look the monster in the eye and live. He lures Cross by reminding him of the deal he offered: 'just find the girl'. The private eye can see that this crippled patriarch is responsible for Mulwray's death as well as Evelyn's death-in-life; Jake knows that the bifocals belonged not to the victim but to the murderer who left his calling card, a mark of split vision in the tide-pool, where the planet's life began and where life ended for the benign Water Commissioner.

But in Cross he is to encounter an adversary whose venality is so far beyond the everyday vices of greed and lust with which Jake is so familiar. Cross has manipulated the water supply not for mere profit but to control the very future. Who could gloss this better than the writer himself?

'That kind of wealth, that kind of greed, is almost an attempt to purchase your own immortality. That's the ultimate vanity and blasphemy about it. If you can control your future that much then that means … you'll never die. That's the unspoken thing here. But I believe guys like that feel that way.'[60]

The split vision of the adversary: capable of anything

Cross cannot feel guilt for what he did to his own estranged daughter. He wants, as if by divine right, to control the destiny not only of the world but also of 'the only daughter I have left ... You see, Mr Gits, most people never have to face the fact that at the right time and in the right place they're capable of anything.'

However compromised Jake may be, swimming in the same water as the rest of us, he is nonetheless, however tarnished, a seeker after truth, a true believer in the ultimate triumph of human rationality. But the rug is finally pulled from under his pursuit of certainty: Noah Cross transcends any mundane political corruption, however far-reaching. He is the very embodiment of the dark side of the human psyche, destructive for destruction's sake, wedded to the irrational, the chaotic, because it is his very nature, because it is our very nature. As a demiurge, the evil creator of a dystopian universe, he is a figure who is not at all out of place in Polanski's middle-European cosmology, though perhaps he seems even more shocking when positioned in the bright sunlight of Towne's Southern Californian hyper-reality.

Jake is out-manoeuvred not just because he is facing an opponent who doesn't play by the same rules, but one who isn't even in the same game and whose transcendent evil has made him untouchable. With the incriminating evidence of the spectacles removed and with a gun to his head, Jake is outwitted and is forced to lead the old man into Chinatown, the very symbol of a state which Cross himself embodies and where, for the rest of us, reason and action does not function.

Speaking at the Edinburgh Film Festival Towne put his finger on the problem: the basic structural decision he had to face was, in his words, 'which scandal do you deal with first?' The political machinations around water and power are, certainly on a societal level, more far-reaching than an isolated act of incest, which is, however, more deeply, outrageously dramatic. 'A man violating his own child is not as serious as a man who is willing to violate everyone's children,' Towne said, but stories, of course, save the most significant revelation till last. 'Maybe it's because America's a puritanical country I felt that the way to drive home the outrage about water and power was to ... cap it with incest.' The rape of the land is not simply mirrored by, it is overtaken by the rape of the daughter.

In choosing to make the revelation of incest, the theme of twisted sexuality, more important than that of political corruption it could be argued that the authors have deflected the historical tale of civic avarice, which was the original springboard for the story, away from the social onto the realm of the ontological. Political critique becomes redundant if, at the end of the tale, there is something so evil in the soul of man that it is impervious to perfectibility. The taint of corruption is exposed not as the measure of a specifically dysfunctional society but, in fact, forms the very foundation of all human interaction.

....

It was Polanski alone who wanted to have Richard Sylbert build a literal Chinatown set on the Paramount back lot so that the metaphorical state could be actualised into a real space in which all the major *dramatis personae* could gather for the finale, like in grand opera. He also, more significantly, argued with Towne (whom he was to ban from the set) about his original ending – a *dénouement* in which Jake rescued Evelyn and the sister/daughter from the clutches of the father/grandfather/rapist; the 'evil tycoon' would be vanquished by Evelyn, who would have her revenge upon him and 'the good guys [would] triumph in the final reel'.[61] Polanski thought 'it was a serious movie, not an adventure story for the kids', but Towne fundamentally disagreed, attributing Polanski's darker vision to his own personal problems: 'Roman's argument was: That's life ... Beautiful blondes die in Los Angeles. Sharon had. He didn't say that but that's what he felt.' Towne would derisively refer to Polanski's ending as 'the tunnel at the end of the light'.[62]

As Polanski tells it he didn't finally decide which ending he was going to shoot until the night before the cameras rolled, but this seems hard to credit. For, as in his previous films *Repulsion* and *Rosemary's Baby*, Polanski's ending retrospectively imbues the whole film with a protective despair which seems to assert that the protagonist's project is not only doomed but laughably naive. Social ills cannot be rectified. Salvation is an illusion. Redemption? Forget it. Evil can never be defeated because it is so deeply engrained into our very being that members of our species find it easier to embrace it than to oppose it.

These oft-repeated tales reflect more than just 'creative disagreements' (the industry's euphemism for 'open hostility'); they reveal fundamentally different world-views. Towne's redemptive possibility would have made the film, in classical terms, a 'comedy',

The patriarchal demiurge triumphant

defined not as something that makes the audience laugh, but as a tale in which love triumphs over the obstacles which stand in its path, where youth defeats age and a new, healthier social order is ultimately achieved. Polanski's pessimistic culmination, however, leads to a reductive circularity, an impossibility of further action that echoes the closure of classical tragedy. In this instance, however, it is tragedy ironically re-configured for the age in which the film was made, a time when America's faith in the Great Society and its leaders had been tested past breaking point.

There are very few commentators on this film who have not 'detected' its structural and thematic resemblance to the story of Oedipus.[63] This seems a hardly insightful archaeological perception as not only has the Theban ruler been the conscious and presiding genius of the detective story ever since Poe consolidated its terms, but Sophocles's hero is also the explicit model for Towne himself who speaks of his own tragic hero as the one who 'determines to find the killer and has him in front of his eyes all along'.

But Jake Gittes is not the one who brought the plague/drought to Thebes/L.A., is he? Is Towne being entirely fair on his creation when he says: 'I think all detective stories are a re-telling of the Oedipus tale. I mean those ... movies where the detective is looking for the solution ... [and] finds he's part of the crime, that he's part of the problem ...'?[64] Sure, Jake's revelations and his concomitant actions only make things worse, but is he really to be implicated in the initial guilty deed? Must the investigating protagonist's hubris in wanting to know, of deluding himself that he can ever really know, be considered as being on a par of existential complicity as the antagonist's wilful and self-serving villainy?

If so, when we (for by now our journey as spectators has fused entirely with that of the investigator) approach Chinatown we are not just crossing into a liminal space – a structural locus which is not just an unstable point on a transition to a future security, however temporary, but is instead a state of mind which is completely impossible to escape, to which we are condemned always to return. We are entering an atonement-free zone, a site in which the possibility of any species of redemption would be laughable, totally out of the question.

Suddenly this commercially viable, industrially successful, fundamentally pleasurable piece of work reveals itself as a most cheerless and subversive appraisal of the society that paid for it to be made: in his own eyes Jake Gittes seems as culpable as Noah Cross – through his moral venality in thinking the worst of Evelyn and in his intellectual vanity which will lead directly to disaster. And we, watching, must share in the guilt.

. . . .

The discordant music and the flashes of neon introduce Chinatown by night: perhaps at this moment the film is most reminiscent of the classic noir and furthest from the classic detective tale. One by one all the major players assemble on the set for this finale immaculately choreographed like the endgame moves of a chess tournament. Jake is flanked by Cross and his heavy, Mulvihill. He sees his operatives, Walsh and Duffy, waiting for him but before he can introduce them they hold up their hands to show they are out of the picture, hand-cuffed. As Escobar enters the frame Jake willingly holds out his own hand to be cuffed: 'good news'. The police are the lesser of two evils, capture by them becomes a liberation from the real villain. But Lou will not listen to Jake's explanation. His protestations that Cross is 'the bird you're after … He's rich. He thinks he can get away with anything,' only result in him being ignored and immobilised by Loach, who, of course, has a personal grudge against Jake, as Cross looks on unperturbed by the forces of law and order. The solution to the crime now means absolutely nothing.

Then Katherine emerges, led by the butler and the maid, in their native milieu. Cross approaches her tenderly, paternally even,

expressing the utter lack of guilt he showed when he told Jake that he didn't blame himself. But he stutters and falters over his words, searching for a correct designation: 'I'm … I'm your gr-grand father, my dear,' then with more confidence: 'I'm your grandfather.' This is no melodramatic villain, no pantomime demon king, but a man who is able to rationalise, if only to himself, even his most depraved behaviour. He is intercepted by Evelyn who sends Curly on with the servants as Cross begs her to be, of all things, 'reasonable'. Clearly that's what this master of chaos thinks that he is being. 'She's mine too,' he pleads, to which Evelyn responds: 'She's never going to know that.'

In this one line the optimistic argument of the detective story and the central mission of its investigator hero are exposed and completely demolished: it is better not to know, some things are better left covered up, repressed. At the very moment when Jake knows everything he is most powerless to act. The bitter Chinatown memory is replayed before his finally all-seeing eyes; the past cannot be transcended, its trauma can never be discharged, its wounds cannot be healed. Jake is little more than an impotent, if not innocent, bystander when he ironically urges Evelyn to 'let the police handle this' as she points a revolver at her perplexed father. Evelyn is well aware of the futility of this advice: 'He owns the police' – the depravity of the social world is irredeemable.

But she, too, is powerless against her father, able only to inflict a flesh wound and Jake cannot prevent Loach shooting after her car. As it comes to a halt in the far distance of a lonely street, the sound of the car horn penetrates the air, an echo of the time Evelyn's head fell forward shortly after Jake had first seen her with Katherine. Jake knows what has happened before this sound is joined by Katherine's screams. The shot has penetrated her eye, the one with the flaw in it, completing the metaphorical cycle of transpositions of images of cracked instruments of seeing, of imperfect vision. Escobar, out of depth in the water he swims in, can only say: 'Turn them all loose,' as Cross leads Katherine away – the very outcome Evelyn's quest was to avoid, an outcome provoked by Jake's naive interference.

Jake is now most like Oedipus at the end of the play, before he puts his own eyes out, no longer able to face the exposed truth his investigation has uncovered. All but destroyed, Jake mutters his final line (another cracked echo) to himself alone: 'As little as possible.' It is not just 'the futility of good intentions' that is informing the state of mind

The liminal zone: 'Forget it, Jake. It's Chinatown'

from which he can never escape, but the futility of *all* action. If, to couple the hydraulic metaphorical system of the film with an obvious Freudian topography, Chinatown is the *id* of the city, the primeval tide-pool ever ready to burst its dam walls and engulf the pavements under the feet of all who stand in its wake, and the hero is the would-be *super-ego* who tries to stick his finger in the dike keeping chaos at bay, then it is finally crystal clear where mastery lies. If the Father (who 'owns the police') is both *id* and *super-ego* what hope remains for the rest of us?

All the last lines, all the final moves, are drenched in tragic irony. Escobar desperately advises Duffy and Walsh to 'just get him the hell out of here,' and tells Jake to 'go home'. As if either course of action were conceivable, let alone simple. Jake's fate is to be forever stuck in liminality, knowing everything, having nothing. He is barely able to stand as he is led into the enveloping darkness, condemned only to repeat.

Walsh's counsel of repression: 'Forget it, Jake. It's Chinatown,' comes far too late and is wishful thinking. 'Chinatown' is precisely what Jake never could forget; if he could, Evelyn would still be alive. The ultimate tragedy is not that he can never wake up from this nightmare but that his actions have also denied the woman he once touched her devoutly wished and his well-planned escape from this cursed waste land. His plague is contagious.

The Chinese residents of Almeda Street, concrete reflection of the audience's own prurient spectatorship, crane their heads forward eager to see more before they are ordered to 'Clear the area!' The story is all but over, the social order into which we will be momentarily returned ('On the sidewalk!', we are ordered) is restored – but not to decency, rationality, love, health and meaning, but to a fundamental, chaotic, unconquerable and unembraceable perversity.

For Chinatown is not the distorted reflection of the world seen through a broken glass darkly, it is the very image of the world.

NOTES

· ·

1 Robert Evans, *The Kid Stays in the Picture*
(London: Aurum Press, 1994), p. 266 – one of
the most egotistical, insightful and enjoyable
accounts of the movie business by an insider
and a survivor.
2 Evans again, of course, *The Kid*, p. 257.
3 Robert Towne, from a BBC TV interview,
Writing Chinatown, first broadcast February
1997.
4 Evans, *The Kid*, p. 258.
5 Raymond Chandler, 'The Simple Art of
Murder' (originally published in 1950) in
Pearls Are a Nuisance (London: Penguin,
1964).
6 A particularly lurid account can be found in
Thomas Kiernan, *Repulsion –The Life and
Times of Roman Polanski* (London: Grove
Press, 1980), p. 29. Perhaps the most awfully
resonant image from this account of the young
Roman's life on the run is his fashioning of a
false foreskin from candle wax so that if he was
caught and strip-searched by the occupying
Nazis, his Jewish identity would be concealed.
7 Evans, *The Kid*, p. 266. For the director's
somewhat different, but no less egomaniacal
take, see Roman Polanski, *Roman on Polanski*
(London: Heinemann, 1984), p. 312.
8 Evans, *The Kid*, p. 257.
9 Peter Biskind, 'The Low Road to
Chinatown', *Premiere*, June 1994, p. 70.
10 Robert Towne, Masterclass on *Chinatown*
at the Edinburgh International Film Festival,
August 1995.
11 Mike Davis, *City of Quartz – Excavating
the Future in Los Angeles* (London: Verso,
1990), p. 18.
12 Polanski, *Roman on Polanski*, p. 303.
13 Towne from a 1989 interview quoted in
Patrick McGilligan, *Jack's Life – A Biography
of Jack Nicholson* (London: Hutchinson,
1994), p. 268.
14 Raymond Chandler, 'Casual Notes on the
Mystery Novel' (written in 1949), in Dorothy
Gardiner and Katherine Sorley Walker (eds),
Raymond Chandler Speaking (Boston:
Houghton Mifflin, 1977).
15 For more information on the earliest
literary detective see my entry on Dupin in

Maxim Jakubowski (ed.), *100 Great Detectives*
(London: Xanadu, 1991), p. 86.
16 Dorothy L. Sayers, Introduction to *Great
Short Stories of Detection, Mystery and Horror*
(London: Gollancz, 1928).
17 Chandler, 'The Simple Art of Murder'.
18 I am using the word 'mythical' here not in
its vernacular usage as an antithesis to reality,
a lie even, but in the more dynamic definition
of Bronislaw Malinowski as 'a charter for
social action'. See *Magic, Science and Religion*
(New York: Doubleday Anchor, 1954),
written in 1925.
19 Polanski, *Roman on Polanksi*, p. 303.
20 *Raymond Chandler Speaking*, p. 233.
21 Hanns Eisler, quoted in Davis, *City of
Quartz*, p. 50.
22 Morrow Mayo, from *Los Angeles*, 1933,
quoted in Davis, *City of Quartz*, p. 33.
23 In his Edinburgh Masterclass Towne said
that he had been inspired by *Southern
California Country: An Island on the Land*
(New York: Duell, Sloane & Pearce, 1946)
by Carey McWilliams, former editor of *The
Nation*, on the Los Angeles water wars, see
chapter X, 'Water! Water! Water!'. The
material contained in this section also leans
heavily on the account in chapter 12 of Remi
Nadeau, *Los Angeles, from Mission to Modern City*
(New York: Longman's Green, 1960) as well
as an article floating around in hyper-space,
'Is "Chinatown" Bad History?' by Kelly
Richmond, December 1996 (which refers
tantalisingly to a 'book in progress' by Catherine
Mulholland, grand-daughter of William).
24 McWilliams, *Southern California*, p.195.
25 Polanski, *Roman on Polanski*, p. 304.
26 This sequence has been fascinatingly
analysed by Anthony Easthope in *What a
Man's Gotta Do* (London: Paladin, 1986),
p. 123 ff as an instance of the way the dirty
joke operates symbolically as an exchange of
women between men and as a type of verbally
displaced scopophilia, the pleasure in looking
at the sexual act (which is, of course, Jake
Gittes's professional m.o.).
27 Evans always had his wife, Ali McGraw, in
the frame for the female lead but by the time

the cameras rolled she had flown the coop and was shacked up with Steve McQueen. Protracted attempts to woo Jane Fonda followed unsuccessfully so Polanski got his choice of Dunaway, despite Evans's reservations about her being 'colder than Baskin-Robbins', Evans, *The Kid*, p. 261 ff.

28 BBC interview, February 1997.

29 See Hitchcock's classic delineation of the differences between 'suspense' and 'shock' in François Truffaut, *Hitchcock by Truffaut* (London: Martin Secker and Warburg, 1968), p. 91.

30 *Raymond Chandler Speaking*, p. 132.

31 Here I am using the conceptual language of Joseph Campbell; see *The Hero with a Thousand Faces* (Princeton: Princeton University Press, 1949; London: Fontana, 1993), p. 77 ff. Campbell's work has become the basis for an approach to screenwriting which is elaborated by Christopher Vogler, former story analyst at Disney, now peripatetic 'how to' guru, in *The Writer's Journey – Mythic Structure for Storytellers and Screenwriters* (Los Angeles: Michael Wiese Productions, 1992).

32 Like the architecture, the wardrobe is so good in this film, defining not only the time of the story but the characters themselves. Anthea Sylbert, the Oscar-nominated costume designer, 'judged that the Los Angeles detective would be influenced in his attire by popular movie star styles. His clothing, she thought, would reflect "an outsider's idea of how a star would dress". Before designing Nicholson's costumes, Sylbert scrutinised period photos of male stars ...' See Barbara Leaming, *Polanski – His Life and Films* (London: Hamish Hamilton, 1982), p. 95.

33 This is what, in Aristotelian terms, would be considered the difference between the *story* and the *plot*: the former term designating the tale's incidents laid out in strict chronological order, the latter being the way they are ordered in the narration of the tale. See Aristotle, *On the Art of Poetry*, trans. T. S. Dorsch (London: Penguin, 1965), especially chapter 6: 'A Description of Tragedy'. So, for instance, the *story* of Oedipus (to pluck any old tale at random) begins before his birth with the Delphic oracle's warning; but the *plot* of *Oedipus Rex* begins with the King of Thebes being confronted with a societal nut he alone can crack.

34 Vladimir Propp, *Morphology of the Folktale* (University of Texas Press, 1975), originally published in 1928.

35 These ideas are dependent upon an entirely undervalued study in the history of structural anthropology and ritual analysis by Arnold van Gennep, *The Rites of Passage* (London: Routledge & Kegan Paul, 1960), first published in French in 1909, as well as a more accessible gloss upon it in Edmund Leach, *Culture and Communication* (Cambridge: Cambridge University Press, 1976).

36 Perhaps more than any other anthropologist, Turner drew out the connections between ritual and drama, arguing indeed, in a lifetime's body of work, for ritual as the *prototype* of drama. See, for instance, *The Ritual Process – Structure and Anti-Structure* (London: Routledge & Kegan Paul, 1969) and *From Ritual to Theatre – The Human Seriousness of Play* (New York: Performing Arts Journal Publications, 1982).

37 In a 'third draft' of the script dated 9 October 1973 a deleted scene is located here which involves an argument between Jake and Lou Escobar where the P.I. accuses the cop of covering up the suspicious circumstances surrounding Mulwray's death 'out of respect for his civic position'. Escobar alludes to the bursting of the dam about which Mulwray had said, in the public meeting: 'I am not making that kind of mistake twice.' Here Lou says: '... [H]e drowned a cousin of mine with about 500 other people. But they weren't very important, just a bunch of dumb Mexicans living by a dam ...' Perhaps it was considered that this social dimension was over-egging an already rich pudding, but its excision leaves Mulwray's earlier statement dangling and un-paid off and its inclusion would have increased sympathy for both the policeman and the water engineer.

38 Polanski, *Roman on Polanski*, p. 310.
39 Ibid., pp. 310–11. Although gossip still
circulates on the Internet that Polanski really
did cut Nicholson's nose, a description of how
the stunt was effected can be found on the
same page.
40 In the third draft of the script Cross's
given name is 'Julian' – doesn't quite have the
same resonance somehow.
41 In another deleted scene Cross's lair is
located on an island to which Jake travels by
plane. The pilot rather too helpfully fills in the
background of Cross's daughter, 'a wild little
thing' who '… ran off to Mexico – rumour
was she was knocked up and didn't even know
who the father was – went there to get rid of
it … Cross was looking for her all over the
country – offered rewards, everything. Felt
real sorry for him, with all his money.'
Whether the scene was shot then dropped or
cut before shooting, we must breathe a sigh of
relief that Jake was denied this knowledge
(and the red herring about getting rid of the
child) in the finished film.
42 An extra-filmic resonance is perhaps
detectable here, as Nicholson had recently
started 'seeing' Huston's daughter, Anjelica.
Of course, at this point in the film Jake has
not yet touched Evelyn, but he still ducks the
question: 'If you want an answer upon that, Mr
Cross, I'll put one of my men upon the job.'
43 Propp, *Morphology of the Folktale*, p. 27.
44 The location, by the way, was in the Simi
Valley, north west of L.A., which is now, true
to the message of the film, almost entirely
incorporated into the relentless suburban
sprawl.
45 Polanski, *Roman on Polanski*, pp. 306–7.
46 Ibid.
47 Ibid.
48 Ibid.
49 Ibid.
50 John A. Alonzo, 'Shooting Chinatown',
American Cinematographer, vol. 56 no. 5, May
1975.

51 Fredric Jameson, 'Postmodernism, or the
Cultural Logic of Late Capitalism', *New Left
Review* 146, July–August 1984.
52 In another deleted scene before Jake
arrives at the orange grove he comes across a
'Rainmaker' with a 'strange machine'
pumping lavender clouds into the air as he
tries to produce a downpour.
53 Towne, Edinburgh Masterclass.
54 Christine Gledhill, 'Klute 1: A
Contemporary Film Noir and Feminist
Criticism', in E. Ann Kaplan (ed.), *Women in
Film Noir* (London: BFI, 1978), p. 18.
55 For a delineation of the term's first use in
1946, derived from the French pulp series
'Série Noire', see Alain Silver and Elizabeth
Ward (eds), *Film Noir – An Encyclopedic
Reference Guide* (London: Bloomsbury, 1980),
p. 1.
56 Most economically outlined in J. A. Place
and L. S. Peterson, 'Some Visual Motifs of
Film Noir', *Film Comment*, vol. 10 no. 1, 1974.
57 Paul Schrader, 'Notes on Film Noir', *Film
Comment*, Spring 1972, pp. 8–13 – he remarks
that '[a]lmost every critic has his own
definition of *film noir*'.
58 Jonathan Benair in Silver and Ward, *Film
Noir*, pp. 56–8. He sees 'Chinatown' as a
metaphor which is 'easily applicable to *film
noir* in general'.
59 Janey Place, 'Women in Film Noir', in
Kaplan, *Women in Film Noir*, p. 35 ff.
60 BBC interview, February 1997.
61 Polanski, *Roman on Polanski*, p. 305.
62 Biskind, *The Low Road to Chinatown*, p. 72.
63 Among their number are R. Barton
Palmer, '*Chinatown* and the Detective Story',
Literature/Film Quarterly, vol. 5 no. 2, Spring
1977, pp. 112–17; Wayne D. MacGinnis,
'*Chinatown*: Roman Polanski's Contemporary
Oedipus Story', *Literature/Film Quarterly*,
vol. 3 no. 3, Summer 1975, pp. 249–51; and
Deborah Linderman, 'Oedipus in Chinatown',
Enclitic, Fall 1981/Spring1982.
64 BBC interview, February 1997.

CREDITS

. . . .

Chinatown

USA
1974
Production Companies
Long Road Productions
A Paramount-Penthouse
presentation
A Robert Evans production
A Roman Polanski film
Producer
Robert Evans
**Associate Producer/
Unit Production
Manager**
C. O. Erickson
**Assistant to the
Producer**
Gary Chazan
Director
Roman Polanski
Assistant Director
Howard W. Koch Jr
**Second Assistant
Director**
Michele Ader
Script Supervisor
May Wale Brown
Casting
Mike Fenton, Jane Feinberg
Screenplay
Robert Towne
Director of Photography
John A. Alonzo
Camera Operator
Hugh Gagnier
Key Grip
Bernie Schwartz
Gaffer
Earl Gilbert
Editor
Sam O'Steen
Assistant Editor
Flo Williamson
Production Designer
Richard Sylbert
Art Director
W. Stewart Campbell
Set Decorator
Ruby Levitt

Set Designers
Gabe Resh, Robert Resh
Prop Master
Bill Mac Sems
Special Effects
Logan Frazee
Costume Designer
Anthea Sylbert
Wardrobe
Richard Bruno, Jean
Merrick
Jewels
The Family Jewels
Make-up
Hank Edds, Lee Harmon
Hairstyles
Susan Germaine, Vivienne
Walker
Titles
Wayne Fitzgerald
Music
Jerry Goldsmith
Music Editor
John C. Hammell
Songs
'I Can't Get Started' by
Vernon Duke, Ira
Gershwin, as recorded by
Bunny Berigan and His
Orchestra; 'Easy Living'
by Leo Robin, Ralph
Rainger; 'The Way You
Look Tonight' by Jerome
Kern, Dorothy Fields;
'Some Day', 'The
Vagabond King Waltz' by
Rudolf Friml, Brian Hooker
Sound Mixer
Larry Jost
Sound Editor
Robert Cornett
Re-recording
Bud Grenzbach
Boom Man
Clint Althaus
**Production Services
Furnished by**
Freedom Service Company

Jack Nicholson
J. J. Gittes
Faye Dunaway
Evelyn Cross Mulwray
John Huston
Noah Cross
Perry Lopez
Lt Lou Escobar
John Hillerman
Yelburton
Darrell Zwerling
Hollis I. Mulwray
Diane Ladd
Ida Sessions
Roy Jenson
Claude Mulvihill
Roman Polanski
man with knife
Dick Bakalyan
Loach
Joe Mantell
Walsh
Bruce Glover
Duffy
Nandu Hinds
Sophie
James O'Reare
lawyer
James Hong
Evelyn's butler
Beulah Quo
the maid
Jerry Fujikawa
the gardener
Belinda Palmer
Katherine
Roy Roberts
Mayor Bagby
Noble Willingham
Elliott Montgomery
councilmen
Rance Howard
irate farmer
George Justin
barber
Doc Erickson
customer

Fritzi Burr
Mulwray's secretary
Charles Knapp
Maury, the mortician
Claudio Martinez
boy on horseback
Federico Roberto
Cross's butler
Allan Warnick
clerk
John Holland
Jesse Vint
Jim Burke
Denny Arnold
farmers in the valley
Burt Young
Curly

Elizabeth Harding
Curly's wife
John Rogers
Mr Palmer
Cecil Elliott
Emma Dill
Paul Jenkins
Lee De Broux
Bob Golden
policemen

11,771 feet
131 minutes

In colour
Technicolor
Panavision

Credits compiled by
Markku Salmi

The print of *Chinatown*
(original theatrical release
version) in the National
Film and Television
Archive was acquired
specially for the 360 Classic
Feature Films project from
Paramount Pictures,
California.

BIBLIOGRAPHY

....

Alonzo, John A., 'Shooting Chinatown', *American Cinematographer*, vol. 56 no. 5, May 1975.

Aristotle, *On the Art of Poetry*, trans. T. S. Dorsch (London: Penguin, 1965).

Biskind, Peter, 'The Low Road to *Chinatown*', *Premiere*, June 1994.

Campbell, Joseph, *The Hero with a Thousand Faces* (Princeton: Princeton University Press, 1949; reprinted London: Fontana, 1993).

Chandler, Raymond, 'The Simple Art of Murder' (originally published in 1950) in *Pearls Are a Nuisance* (London: Penguin, 1964).

—————'Casual Notes on the Mystery Novel' (written in 1949), in *Raymond Chandler Speaking*, (eds) Dorothy Gardiner and Katherine Sorley Walker (Boston: Houghton Mifflin, 1977).

Davis, Mike, *City of Quartz – Excavating the Future in Los Angeles* (London: Verso, 1990).

Easthope, Anthony, *What a Man's Gotta Do* (London: Paladin, 1986).

Evans, Robert, *The Kid Stays in the Picture* (London: Aurum Press, 1994).

Jakubowski, Maxim (ed.), *100 Great Detectives* (London: Xanadu, 1991).

Jameson, Fredric, 'Postmodernism, or the Cultural Logic of Late Capitalism', *New Left Review* 146, July–August, 1984.

Kaplan, E. Ann (ed.), *Women in Film Noir* (London: BFI, 1978).

Kiernan, Thomas, *Repulsion – The Life and Times of Roman Polanski* (London: Grove Press, 1980).

Leach, Edmund, *Culture and Communication* (Cambridge: Cambridge University Press, 1976).

Leaming, Barbara, *Polanski – His Life and Films* (London: Hamish Hamilton, 1982).

Linderman, Deborah, 'Oedipus in *Chinatown*', *Enclitic*, Fall 1981/Spring1982.

MacGinnis, Wayne D., '*Chinatown*: Roman Polanski's Contemporary Oedipus Story', *Literature/Film Quarterly*, vol. 5 no. 2, Spring 1977, pp. 112–17.

McGilligan, Patrick, *Jack's Life – A Biography of Jack Nicholson* (London: Hutchinson, 1994).

McWilliams, Carey, *Southern California Country: An Island on the Land* (New York: Duell, Sloane & Pearce, 1946).

Nadeau, Remi, *Los Angeles, from Mission to Modern City* (New York: Longman's Green, 1960).

Palmer, R. Barton, '*Chinatown* and the Detective Story', *Literature/Film Quarterly*, vol. 3 no. 3, Summer 1975, pp. 249–51.

Place, J. A. and L. S. Peterson, 'Some Visual Motifs of Film Noir', *Film Comment*, vol. 10 no. 1, 1974.

Polanski, Roman, *Roman on Polanski* (London: Heinemann, 1984).

Propp, Vladimir, *Morphology of the Folktale* (Austin: University of Texas Press, 1975).

Sayers, Dorothy L., Introduction to *Great Short Stories of Detection, Mystery and Horror* (London: Gollancz, 1928).

Schrader, Paul, 'Notes on Film Noir', *Film Comment*, Spring 1972, pp. 8–13.

Silver, Alain and Elizabeth Ward (eds), *Film Noir – An Encyclopedic Reference Guide* (London: Bloomsbury, 1980).

Turner, Victor, *From Ritual to Theatre – The Human Seriousness of Play* (New York: Performing Arts Journal Publications, 1982).

—————*The Ritual Process – Structure and Anti-Structure* (London: Routledge & Kegan Paul, 1969).

Truffaut, François, *Hitchcock by Truffaut* (London: Martin Secker and Warburg, 1968).

van Gennep, Arnold, *The Rites of Passage* (London: Routledge & Kegan Paul, 1960), English trans., first published in French in 1909.

Vogler, Christopher, *The Writer's Journey – Mythic Structure for Storytellers and Screenwriters* (Los Angeles: Michael Wiese Productions, 1992).

ALSO PUBLISHED

If you would like further information about future BFI Film Classics or about other books on film, media and popular culture from BFI Publishing, please write to:

BFI Film Classics
BFI Publishing
21 Stephen Street
London W1P 2LN